A QUICK COURSE IN

LOTUS 1-2-3®

Release 4 for Windows

JOYCE COX

PATRICK KERVRAN

JOYCE COUSINEAU

AN ONLINE PRESS BOOK

PUBLISHED BY
Online Press Incorporated
14320 NE 21st Street, Suite 18
Bellevue, WA 98007
(206) 641-3434, (800) 854-3344

Publisher's Cataloging in Publication
(Prepared by Quality Books Inc.)

Cox, Joyce.
  A quick course in Lotus 1-2-3 release 4 for Windows / Joyce K.
Cox, Patrick Kervran, Joyce Cousineau.
  p. cm.
  Includes index.
  ISBN 1-879399-20-2

  1. 1-2-3 for Windows. 2. Electronic spreadsheets. 3. Windows
(Computer programs) I. Kervran, Patrick. II. Cousineau, Joyce.
III. Title.

HF5548.4.L67C6 1993   650'.0285'5369
                               QBI93-1190

                                    93-085718
                                    CIP

Printed and bound in the United States of America.

  2 3 4 5 6 7 8 9 L O O L 3 2 1 0

Other Quick Course® books

Contents

1

Building a Simple Worksheet

What you will learn

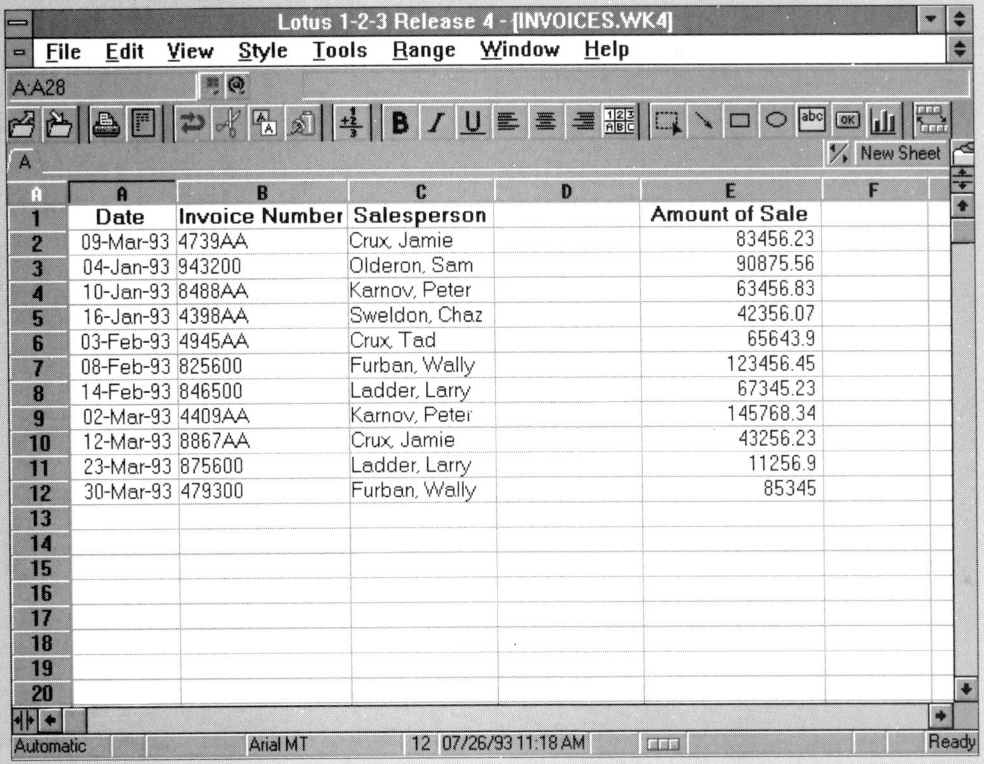

Lotus 1-2-3 Release 4 - [INVOICES.WK4]

File　Edit　View　Style　Tools　Range　Window　Help

A:A28

New Sheet

	A	B	C	D	E	F
1	Date	Invoice Number	Salesperson		Amount of Sale	
2	09-Mar-93	4739AA	Crux, Jamie		83456.23	
3	04-Jan-93	943200	Olderon, Sam		90875.56	
4	10-Jan-93	8488AA	Karnov, Peter		63456.83	
5	16-Jan-93	4398AA	Sweldon, Chaz		42356.07	
6	03-Feb-93	4945AA	Crux, Tad		65643.9	
7	08-Feb-93	825600	Furban, Wally		123456.45	
8	14-Feb-93	846500	Ladder, Larry		67345.23	
9	02-Mar-93	4409AA	Karnov, Peter		145768.34	
10	12-Mar-93	8867AA	Crux, Jamie		43256.23	
11	23-Mar-93	875600	Ladder, Larry		11256.9	
12	30-Mar-93	479300	Furban, Wally		85345	
13						
14						
15						
16						
17						
18						
19						
20						

Automatic　　Arial MT　　12　07/26/93 11:18 AM　　Ready

You're probably sitting at your computer, anxious to start crunching numbers. But before we start, we need to cover some basics, such as how to enter text and numbers, save files, move around a worksheet, edit and format entries, and print the results of your labors. After we discuss a few fundamentals, you'll easily be able to create the worksheets and charts we cover in the rest of the book.

We assume that you've already installed Windows version 3.0 or later and Lotus 1-2-3 Release 4 for Windows on your computer. We also assume that you've worked with Windows before and that you know how to start programs, move windows, choose commands from menus, highlight text, and so on. If you are a Windows novice, we recommend that you take a look at *A Quick Course in Windows*, another book in the Quick Course series, which will help you quickly come up to speed.

To follow the instructions in this book, you must be using a mouse. Although it is theoretically possible to work in Windows and 1-2-3 using just the keyboard, we would not wish this fate on anyone, and most of our instructions involve using a mouse. Occasionally, however, when it is easier or faster to use the keyboard, we give the keyboard equivalent of the mouse action.

Let's get going. With the DOS prompt (C:\>) on your screen, start Windows by typing *win* and pressing Enter. Then in

No Lotus Applications group?

The Lotus 1-2-3 for Windows installation program creates the Lotus Applications group by default. If you don't have a Lotus Applications group, someone might have moved the 1-2-3 files to a different group. Open other group windows, locate the Lotus 1-2-3 Release 4 icon, and double-click it to start the program.

Other ways of starting

To start 1-2-3 (or any other Windows program) directly from the DOS prompt, type *win*, a space, and the path and name of the program. For example, type *win 123r4w\programs\123w*, and press Enter. After loading Program Manager, Windows starts 1-2-3. You can also start 1-2-3 with a worksheet already loaded by typing *win*, the path and name of the program, and the worksheet's filename.

Icons for your worksheets

You can create icons for worksheets in Program Manager so that you can start 1-2-3 with a frequently used worksheet already loaded. Simply make a copy of the Lotus 1-2-3 Release 4 icon, highlight the icon, and choose Properties from the File menu. Then add the worksheet's name to the entry in the Command Line edit box and adjust the Description entry.

Windows, start 1-2-3 by double-clicking the Lotus 1-2-3 ←
Release 4 icon in the Lotus Applications group window.

Starting Lotus 1-2-3

Getting Oriented

When you start 1-2-3 for the first time, your screen looks
something like this:

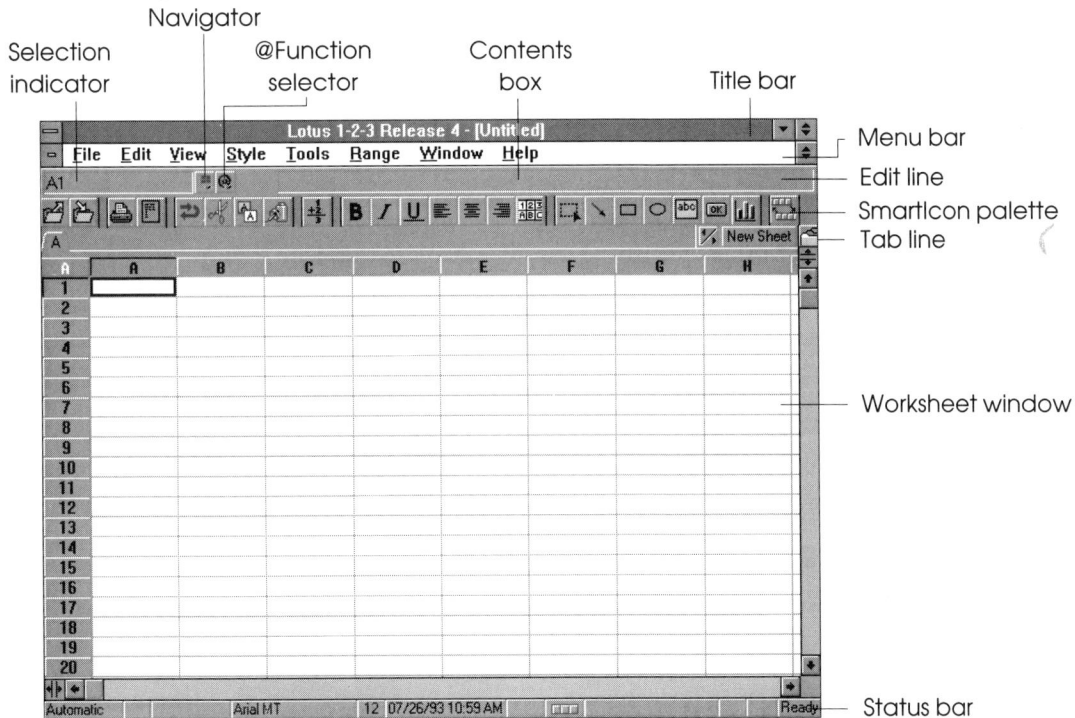

At the top of the screen is the 1-2-3 for Windows *title bar*,
and below that is the *menu bar*, from which you choose
commands. Below the menu bar is the *edit line*, which contains the following:

- The *selection indicator* tells you where on the worksheet you
  are currently working.

- The *navigator* lists the range names created for the current
  worksheet. (Range names are discussed on page 41.)

- The *@function selector* displays a list of @functions available for use in formulas. (See page 39 and 52 for information
  about @functions.)

- The *contents box* displays the entries you make in the cells of
  the worksheet.

Clicking and double-clicking

Clicking is a simple matter of
pressing and releasing the mouse
button once. To double-click, you
quickly click the mouse button
twice. If double-clicking doesn't
produce the anticipated result, try
again, this time clicking a little
faster.

Below the edit line is the *SmartIcon palette*, which puts a host of often-used commands and features within easy reach. The default SmartIcon palette—the one shown on the previous page—is one of eight predefined palettes available in 1-2-3.

The blank worksheet takes up the majority of the screen, which as you can see, is laid out in a grid of *columns* and *rows* like the ledger paper used by accountants. There are 256 columns, lettered A through IV, and 8192 rows, numbered 1 through 8192. The rectangle at the junction of each column and row is called a *cell*. To identify each of the 2,097,152 cells on the worksheet, 1-2-3 uses an *address*, or *reference*, that consists of the letter at the top of the cell's column and the number at the left end of its row. For example, the reference of the cell in the top left corner of the worksheet is A1. The *active cell*—the one you are working with—is designated on the worksheet by a frame called the *cell pointer*. 1-2-3 displays the reference of the active cell in the selection indicator.

Cell references

A single 1-2-3 worksheet file can contain up to 256 sheets, lettered A through IV. The letter identifier is displayed on a *sheet tab* in the *tab line* below the SmartIcon palette. When you are working with multiple sheets, 1-2-3 also displays the sheet identifier along with the cell reference in the selection indicator. For example, A:A1 is the cell in the top left corner of sheet A of the current worksheet file. When you are working in a worksheet file that contains only one sheet— sheet A—you can safely use cell references without the sheet letter. (For more about using multiple sheets, see page 28.)

Multiple sheets

At the bottom of the screen, the *status bar* displays useful information about number and text formats, the date and time, SmartIcon palettes and other conditions.

Entering Labels

Most worksheets consist of blocks of text and numbers in table format on which you can perform various calculations. In 1-2-3, text entries are known as *labels* and numeric entries are known as *values*. To make your worksheets easy to decipher, you usually enter labels as column and row headings that describe the associated entries. Let's try entering a few headings now:

Entering headings

1. With the cell pointer on cell A1 of the worksheet, type *Date*. As you type, the text appears in both the cell and the contents box, and a blinking insertion point in the cell tells you where the next character you type will be inserted. A Confirm button (✓) and Cancel button (✗) appear between the @function selector and contents box. Meanwhile, the mode indicator at the right end of the status bar changes from Ready to Label, because 1-2-3 recognizes this entry as a label.

The Confirm and Cancel buttons

2. Click the Confirm button to complete the entry. 1-2-3 enters the Date heading in cell A1, and the mode indicator changes to Ready. Notice that the entry is left-aligned in its cell. Unless you tell 1-2-3 to do otherwise, it always left-aligns labels.

3. Click cell B1 to select it. The cell pointer moves to the newly selected cell, and the reference displayed in the selection indicator changes from A1 to B1.

4. Type *Invoice Number*, but instead of clicking the Confirm button to enter the heading in the cell, press the Right Arrow key. 1-2-3 completes the entry in cell B1 and moves the cell pointer to C1.

5. Type *Salesperson* and press the Right Arrow key.

6. Now enter one more heading. In cell D1, type *Amount of Sale* and click Confirm to complete the entry. Here's how the worksheet looks with the newly entered row of headings:

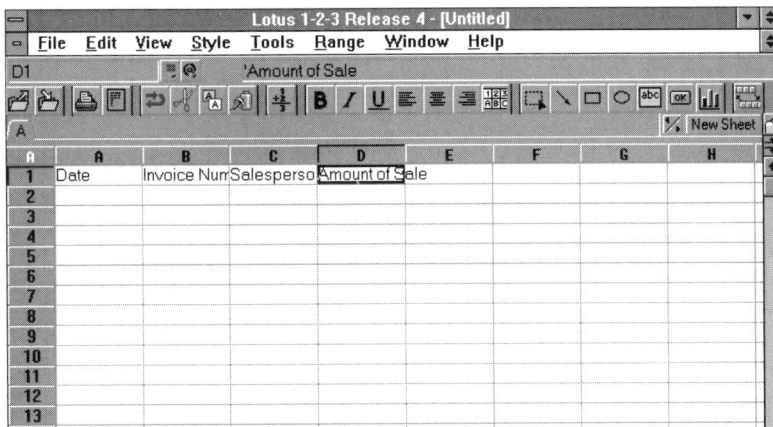

Mouse pointer shapes

The mouse pointer takes on different shapes depending on its location on the screen. For example, the pointer becomes an arrow when it is over the worksheet, a menu, a SmartIcon, or a title bar; a double-headed arrow when it is over a column or row header border; and an I-beam when it is over the contents box.

Notice that the headings in cells B1, C1, and D1 are too long to fit in their cells. Until you entered the Salesperson heading in cell C1, the Invoice Number heading spilled over into C1, just as Amount of Sale now spills over from D1 into E1. After you entered the Salesperson heading, 1-2-3 truncated Invoice Number so that you could read the heading in C1. The Invoice Number and Salesperson headings are still intact, however. (If you're skeptical, click either cell and look at the contents box.) Later in this chapter, you'll learn how to adjust column widths to accommodate long entries (see page 27).

That completes the column headings. Now let's turn our attention to the rest of the table. We'll skip the Date and Invoice Number columns for now and enter the names of a few salespeople in last-name/first-name order in column C.

1. Click cell C2 and type *Crux, Jamie.*

2. Instead of clicking the Confirm button, press the Down Arrow key. 1-2-3 completes the entry in C2 and moves the cell pointer to C3.

3. In cell C3, type *Olderon, Sam* and press the Down Arrow key to complete the entry and move to cell C4.

4. Next, type the following names in the Salesperson column, pressing the Down Arrow key after each one:

C4	Karnov, Peter
C5	Swelden, Chaz
C6	Crux, Tad
C7	Furban, Wally
C8	Ladder, Larry
C9	Karnov, Peter
C10	Crux, Jamie
C11	Ladder, Larry
C12	Furban, Wally

Correcting mistakes

If you make a mistake, select the cell containing the error and press F2 to activate the edit line, or double-click the cell to edit it directly. Press Home or End to move the insertion point to the beginning or end of the entry, and press Right Arrow or Left Arrow to move the insertion point forward or backward one character. Press Backspace or Delete to delete the character before or after the insertion point.

Entering Numbers as Labels

Now let's enter the invoice numbers in column B. Normally, you will want 1-2-3 to treat invoice numbers—and social security numbers, part numbers, phone numbers, and other numbers that are used primarily for identification—as labels rather than as values on which you might want to perform calculations. If the "number" includes not only the digits 0 through 9 but also letters and other characters (such as hyphens), 1-2-3 usually recognizes it as a label. However, if the number consists of only digits and you want 1-2-3 to treat it as a label, you have to explicitly tell 1-2-3 to do so.

For demonstration purposes, assume that your company has two regional offices, East and West. Both offices use invoice numbers with six characters. Invoices generated by the East office consist of four digits followed by the letters AA, and those generated by the West office consist of six digits that end with 00 (two zeros). Follow these steps to see how 1-2-3 treats these invoice numbers:

1. Click cell B2, type *4739AA* and press Down Arrow. This invoice number consists of both digits and letters, so 1-2-3 treats the entry as text and left-aligns it.

2. In cell B3, which is now active, type *943200* and press Enter. This invoice number consists of only digits, so 1-2-3 treats the entry as a value and right-aligns it in its cell.

How do you tell 1-2-3 to treat an entry that consists of only digits as a label? You begin the entry with a single quote mark ('). Follow these steps:

Using single quote marks

1. In cell B3, type *'943200* and press Enter. (When you type the new entry, 1-2-3 overwrites the old entry.) Because of the single quote mark, 1-2-3 recognizes the new entry as a label.

2. Enter these invoice numbers as labels in the indicated cells, preceding those that end in 00 with a single quote mark:

B4	8488AA
B5	4398AA
B6	4945AA
B7	'825600
B8	'846500
B9	4409AA
B10	8867AA
B11	'875600
B12	'479300

Lotus 1-2-3 Release 4 - [Untitled]

File   Edit   View   Style   Tools   Range   Window   Help

B13

	A	B	C	D	E	F	G	H
1	Date	Invoice Num	Salesperso	Amount of Sale				
2		4739AA	Crux, Jamie					
3		943200	Olderon, Sam					
4		8488AA	Karnov, Peter					
5		4398AA	Sweldon, Chaz					
6		4945AA	Crux, Tad					
7		825600	Furban, Wally					
8		846500	Ladder, Larry					
9		4409AA	Karnov, Peter					
10		8867AA	Crux, Jamie					
11		875600	Ladder, Larry					
12		479300	Furban, Wally					
13								

Long numeric values

1-2-3 allows a long text entry to overflow into an adjacent empty cell and truncates the entry only if the adjacent cell also contains an entry. However, the program treats a long numeric value differently. If 1-2-3 displays asterisks (*) instead of the value you entered, the value is too large to display in the cell, and you must make the column wider to view it. By default, values are displayed in scientific notation, and values with many decimal places might be rounded. For example, if you enter 12345678912345 in a cell with standard width (which holds 9 characters), 1-2-3 displays 1.2E+13 (1.2 times 10 to the 13th power). If you enter 123456.789 in a standard-width cell, 1-2-3 displays 123456.8. In both cases, 1-2-3 leaves the underlying value unchanged, and you can widen the column to display the value in the format in which you entered it. (Adjusting the width of columns is discussed on page 27.)

Entering Values

As you have seen, entering numeric values is just as easy as entering labels. Follow along with the next few steps as we enter the sales amounts in column D:

1. Click cell D2 to select the first cell in the Amount of Sale column and type *83456.23*. Notice that the mode indicator displays the word Value. Press Down Arrow to complete the entry; which 1-2-3 right-aligns in its cell.

2. Enter the following amounts in the indicated cells, pressing Down Arrow after each one:

D3	90875.56
D4	634568.30
D5	42356.07
D6	65643.90
D7	123456.45
D8	67345.23
D9	145768.34
D10	43256.23
D11	11256.90
D12	85345.00

Don't worry if 1-2-3 does not display these values exactly as you entered them (see the adjacent tip). On page 48, we format these amounts so that they display as dollars and cents.

Entering Dates and Times

Even seasoned 1-2-3 users sometimes have difficulty entering dates and times in their worksheets. For a date or time to be displayed correctly, you must enter it "in format," meaning that you must enter it in a format that 1-2-3 recognizes as a date or time. 1-2-3 then displays the entry as you want it but stores it as a value so that you can conveniently perform date and time arithmetic. The following formats are recognized:

Date and time formats

3/9/93	9:35 PM
9-Mar-93	9:35:43 PM
9-Mar	9:35
Mar-93	

Two additional formats combine both date and time and take these forms:

3/9/93 9:35   3-9-93 9:35

Let's see how 1-2-3 handles different date formats:

1. Enter the following dates in the indicated cells, pressing the Down Arrow key after each one. Don't worry if 1-2-3 displays the dates differently from the way you enter them. Later, we'll come back and clean up the Date column so that the dates all appear in the same format.

A2	9-Mar-93
A3	1/4/93
A4	10-Jan-93
A5	16-Jan-93
A6	3-Feb-93
A7	2/8/93
A8	2/14/93
A9	3/2/93
A10	3/12/93
A11	23-Mar-93
A12	30-Mar-93

As you can see on the next page, you've now completed all the columns of this simple worksheet.

Selecting Ranges

Well, we've created a basic worksheet. But before we can show you some of the things you can do with it, we first need to discuss how to select blocks of cells, called *ranges*. Any rectangular block or blocks containing more than one cell is a range. A range can include two cells, an entire row or column, or the entire worksheet. Knowing how to select and work with ranges saves you time, because you can apply formats to or reference the whole range, instead of dealing with each cell individually. Range references consist of the address of the cell in the top left corner of the rectangular block and the address of the cell in the bottom right corner, separated by two periods. For example, A1..B2 identifies the range that consists of cells A1, A2, B1 and B2.

The simplest way to learn how to select ranges is to actually do it, so follow these steps:

1. Point to cell A1, hold down the mouse button, and drag diagonally to cell D12 without releasing the button. 1-2-3 attaches two "cells" to the arrow pointer to indicate that you are selecting a range and highlights the block as you drag.

2. Release the mouse button when the range A1..D12 is highlighted. 1-2-3 displays the range reference in the selection indicator. As you can see here, cell A1—the cell where you started the selection—is white, indicating that it is the active cell in the range.

Range references

Selecting more than one block

A range can consist of more than one block of cells. Multi-block ranges are known as *collections*. To create a collection, select the first range and then hold down the Ctrl key and select the next range, and so on.

Next, try selecting ranges with the keyboard:

1. Select cell B6, hold down the Shift key, press the Right Arrow key twice and the Down Arrow key twice, and release the Shift key. The range B6..D8 is selected.

   Selecting with the keyboard

2. Press the Esc key to deselect the range. The cell pointer remains at B6, which is still the active cell.

Giving 1-2-3 Instructions

Now that you know how to select cells and ranges, let's quickly cover how you tell 1-2-3 what it should do with your selection.

Using Menus

You usually give 1-2-3 instructions by choosing *commands* that are arranged in *menus* on the menu bar. Because this procedure is the same for all Windows applications, we assume that you are familiar with it and provide only a quick review here. If you are a new Windows user, we suggest that you spend a little time becoming familiar with the mechanics of menus, commands, and dialog boxes before proceeding.

To choose a command from a menu, you first click the menu in the menu bar. When the menu drops down, you simply click the name of the command you want. To do the same thing from the keyboard, you can press the Alt key to activate the menu bar, press the underlined letter of the name of the menu, and then press the underlined letter of the command you want.

Choosing commands

Cascade menus

Some command names are followed by an arrowhead, indicating that a *cascade menu*, or *submenu*, will appear when you choose that command. You choose commands from submenus just like commands from regular menus.

Dialog boxes

Some command names are followed by an ellipsis (...), indicating that you must supply more information before 1-2-3 can carry out the command. When you choose one of these commands, 1-2-3 displays a *dialog box*. You can then give the necessary information by typing in an *edit box* or by selecting options from *list boxes* and clicking *check boxes* and *option buttons*. (Most dialog boxes have a Help button that provides information about the dialog box and how to complete its edit boxes and select its options.) You close the dialog box and carry out the command according to your specifications by clicking a *command button*—usually OK. Clicking Cancel closes the dialog box and cancels the command. Other command buttons might be available to refine the original command or to open other dialog boxes.

Unavailable commands

Some command names are occasionally displayed in gray letters, indicating that you can't choose those commands. For example, the Paste command on the Edit menu appears in gray until you have used the Cut or Copy command.

As a short example of how to use menu commands and dialog boxes, follow these steps to apply a display format to the dates you entered in column A of your worksheet:

1. Use the mouse or keyboard to select the range A2..A12, which contains the dates.

2. Click Style on the menu bar to drop down the Style menu.

3. Click Number Format to display this dialog box:

Help with commands

If you can't remember the name of the command you want to use, you can pull down each menu and press the Up Arrow and Down Arrow keys to highlight each command in turn. A brief description of the highlighted command appears in the window's title bar.

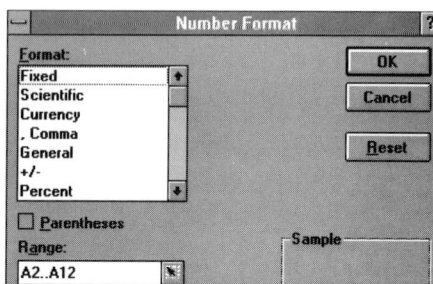

Notice that the edit box in the bottom left corner displays A2..A12, the range you selected.

4. Click the down arrow at the bottom of the Format list box's scroll bar until 31-Dec-93, the first of several available date formats, is in view.

5. Click 31-Dec-93 to select it, and then click OK to close the dialog box and apply the format to the selected cells.

6. Press the Home key to move the cell pointer to A1. 1-2-3 displays all the dates in the same format, as shown here:

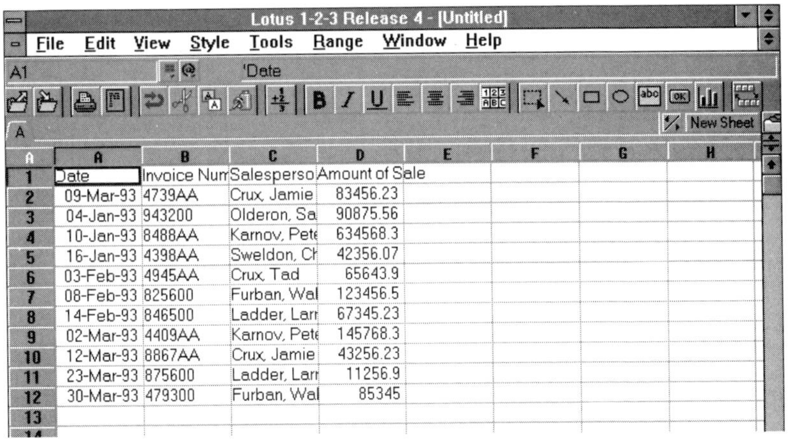

We discuss some of the other formats available in the Number Format dialog box on page 48.

Using Quick Menus

Quick menus are context-sensitive menus that group together the commands used frequently with a specific type of object, such as a cell or a chart element. You display the quick menu by pointing to the object and clicking the right mouse button. You can then choose a command from the menu in the usual way. We'll use quick menus whenever they are the most efficient method of giving 1-2-3 instructions.

Using 1-2-3's Classic Menu

If you have experience with an earlier DOS version of Lotus 1-2-3, you might want to use an alternate menu system, known as the *1-2-3 Classic menu*, which appears on the screen when you press the Forward Slash key (/).

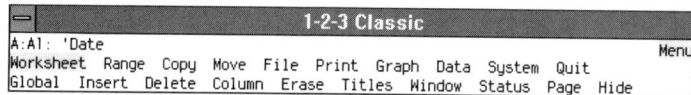

```
                         1-2-3 Classic
A:A1: 'Date                                                      Menu
Worksheet  Range  Copy  Move  File  Print  Graph  Data  System  Quit
Global  Insert  Delete  Column  Erase  Titles  Window  Status  Page  Hide
```

To close the 1-2-3 Classic menu without choosing a command, you press the Esc key. Because the 1-2-3 Classic menu seems familiar and comfortable, DOS 1-2-3 users might want to access this menu occasionally while learning Lotus 1-2-3 for Windows. In the long run, however, you'll be better off if you master the Windows-style menus.

Using SmartIcons

Another way to give instructions is by clicking icons on the SmartIcon palette. 1-2-3 comes with eight built-in SmartIcon palettes: Default Sheet, Editing, Formatting, Goodies, Macro, Printing, Auditing, and Working Together. You can customize these palettes to suit your needs, and you can create your own. By default, 1-2-3 displays the Default Sheet palette, but you can display a different palette at any time. Here's how to cycle through the available palettes using the SmartIcon icon:

Displaying other palettes

1. Click the SmartIcon icon to display this Editing palette:

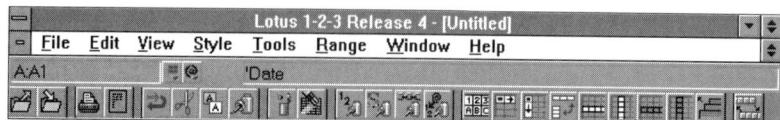

The Default Sheet SmartIcon palette

The Default Sheet SmartIcon palette puts these helpful tools at your fingertips (from left to right):

Open opens an existing worksheet, and **Save** saves the current worksheet.

Print prints the current selection or worksheet, and **Preview** displays a print preview of the worksheet.

Undo reverses an action, and **Cut**, **Copy**, and **Paste** perform cut-and-paste and copy-and-paste operations.

Sum enters one or more @SUM formulas into your worksheet.

Bold, **Italic**, and **Underline** apply styles.

The three **Alignment** icons change the alignment of labels in a cell or range.

Range Fill fills in a selected range sequentially.

Lasso selects several objects at one time.

The four **Draw** icons select and draw objects on the worksheet.

Macro places a button on your worksheet to which you can attach a macro.

Chart plots a chart of the selected worksheet values on the worksheet.

SmartIcon displays the next palette of icons.

2. Browse through the available palettes by clicking the SmartIcon icon a few more times.

3. Click the SmartIcon selector on the status bar to display the palette quick menu, which lists the available palettes and allows you to hide the palette completely.

Selecting a palette

4. Choose Default Sheet from the quick menu to restore the original palette.

5. Hide the SmartIcon palette by clicking the SmartIcon selector on the status bar and choosing Hide SmartIcons from the bottom of the quick menu.

Hiding the palette

6. Redisplay the palette by clicking the SmartIcon selector and choosing Show SmartIcons from the quick menu.

Using Accelerator Keys

If you and your mouse don't get along and you prefer to use the keyboard, you can access many 1-2-3 commands by means of keyboard shortcuts called *accelerator keys*. The list of these keys is extensive and would take a lot of space to reproduce here. You can find information about them by choosing the Keyboard command from the Help menu. (For more information about the Lotus 1-2-3 Help system, see page 32.)

Creating palettes

After you become comfortable using the predefined palettes, you might want to create your own. Choose the SmartIcons command from the Tools menu to display a dialog box in which you can change the icons on an existing palette or save a combination of icons as a new palette. You can also enlarge and edit the icons associated with particular commands in this dialog box.

Customizing the palette

You can move the SmartIcon palette by choosing SmartIcons from the Tools menu and selecting the desired position in the Position box. When you click OK, 1-2-3 moves the palette to the selected position.

Help with SmartIcons

To view a brief description of any SmartIcon, point to the icon and hold down the right mouse button. The description appears in the title bar and remains there as long as you hold down the button. You can also get information about the SmartIcon equivalents of the menu commands by choosing Contents from the Help menu and then selecting SmartIcons Reference.

Saving Worksheets

Let's return to the worksheet we have created and find out how to save it for future use. As you'll see if you follow these steps, the first time you save a worksheet, you must give its file a name:

Naming worksheets

1. Choose Save As from the File menu to display the Save As dialog box (you can also click the Save icon):

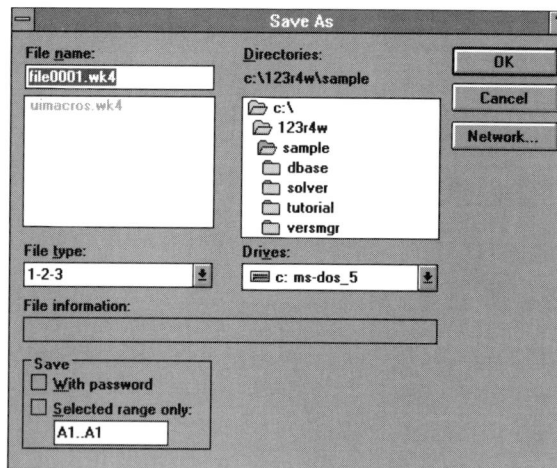

2. Type *invoices* to replace the suggested filename. There's no need to supply an extension because 1-2-3 automatically uses WK4 to indicate that the file is a Release 4 worksheet.

3. Leave the other settings in the dialog box as they are for now, and click OK to carry out the command.

File-naming conventions

DOS file-naming conventions apply to 1-2-3 worksheet names. The names you assign your worksheets must be eight characters or less and can include letters, numbers and the following characters:

_ ^ $! # % & - { } ( )

They cannot contain spaces, commas, or periods.

A different directory

By default, worksheets are saved in 123R4W\SAMPLE. To save a worksheet in a different directory, simply select the directory you want from the Directories list box in the Save As dialog box before clicking OK. You can specify a different default directory by choosing User Setup from the Tools menu and entering the desired directory's path and name in the Worksheet Directory edit box.

Password protection

You can assign a password of up to 15 characters to a worksheet file. Click the With Password check box in the Save As dialog box, and then click OK to display a new dialog box in which you must type the password twice. 1-2-3 will then require that the password be entered correctly before it will open the worksheet.

When you return to the 1-2-3 window, notice that the name INVOICES.WK4 has replaced Untitled in the worksheet's title bar.

From now on, you can save this worksheet by choosing Save from the File menu instead of Save As. 1-2-3 then saves the worksheet by overwriting the previous version with the new version. If you want to save the changes you have made to a worksheet but preserve the previous version, you can assign the new version a different name by choosing the Save As command, entering the new filename, and clicking OK.

Saving existing worksheets

Preserving the previous version

Creating New Worksheets

Having saved the worksheet, let's create a new one so that we can see how to work with more than one file at the same time:

1. Choose New from the File menu. 1-2-3 opens a new worksheet window titled FILE0001.WK4.

That's all there is to it. Although you can see only one worksheet at the moment, you now have two open worksheets with which to experiment.

Manipulating Windows

Let's take a moment to review some window basics. Being able to work with more than one worksheet open at a time is useful, especially if you frequently need to use the same set of numbers in different worksheets. For example, you might use the same raw data to develop a budget or work out a trial balance or create an income statement. Follow these steps to see how easy it is to move from one worksheet to another:

1. Click Window in the menu bar to drop down the Window menu. Notice that the names of the two open worksheets appear at the bottom of the menu. A check mark indicates the active worksheet.

Displaying another open worksheet

2. Choose INVOICES.WK4 from the bottom of the Window menu. The two worksheets switch places so that INVOICES now hides FILE0001.

Arranging windows →

3. Choose Tile from the Window menu. 1-2-3 arranges the two worksheets so that they each occupy half the screen, like this:

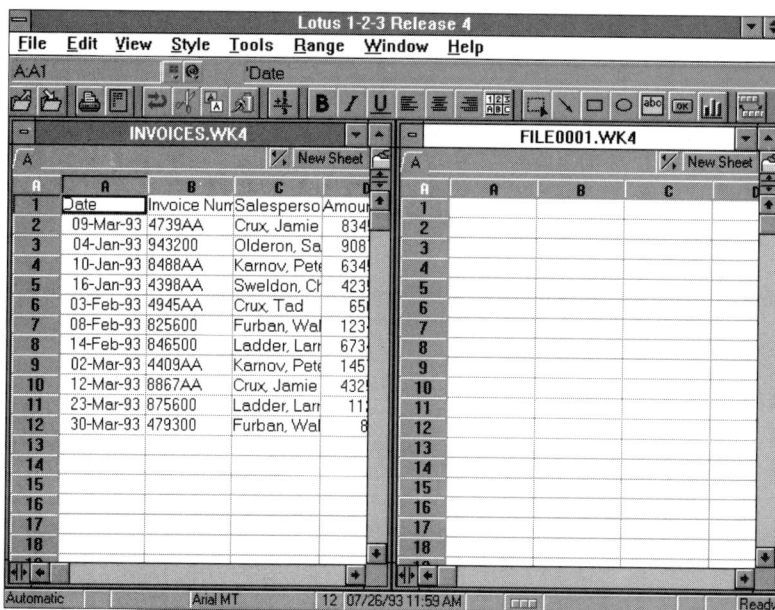

4. Click anywhere in FILE0001 to make it the active worksheet. Notice that the color of its title bar changes to indicate that it is active. Any entries you make and any commands you choose will now affect this worksheet.

Maximizing windows →

5. Click the active window's Maximize button (the upward-pointing arrowhead in the top right corner of FILE0001's title bar). FILE0001 expands to fill the screen, completely hiding INVOICES, and its name is now displayed in square brackets in the title bar.

6. We will work with INVOICES in the next section, so choose this worksheet from the Window menu.

These simple techniques work equally well whether you have two worksheets open or several.

Moving Around

The fastest way to move around the worksheet is with the mouse. As you've seen, clicking any cell moves the cell pointer to that location and displays a new reference in the selection indicator at the left end of the edit line. To display parts of the worksheet that are currently out of sight, you can use the scroll bars, which function the same way as scroll bars in all Windows applications. Try this:

1. With the cell pointer on A1 in INVOICES.WK4, click the arrows at the bottom of the vertical scroll bar and the right end of the horizontal scroll bar until cell P37 comes into view.

2. Press the Home key to jump back to cell A1.

Jumping to cell A1

As you know, you can also use the keyboard to move around the worksheet. The keys you'll probably use most often are the four Arrow keys, but as you gain more experience with 1-2-3, you might find other keys useful. Here's a list of navigation keys and what they do:

To do this ...	Press ...
Scroll right one window width	Ctrl-Right Arrow or Tab
Scroll left one window width	Ctrl-Left Arrow or Shift-Tab
Scroll down one window length	PgDn or Page Down
Scroll up one window length	PgUp or Page Up
Move to end of active area	End then Ctrl-Home
Move to cell A1	Home

Another way to move around the worksheet is with the Go To command. Try this:

1. Choose Go To from the Edit menu to display this dialog box:

Jumping to a specific cell

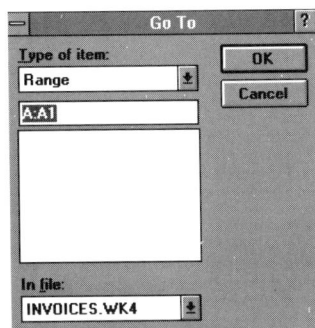

2. Type the reference of the cell that you want to go to. For this example, type *Z46* in the edit box, and click OK. Immediately, 1-2-3 scrolls the worksheet and moves the cell pointer to Z46.

3. Press Home to return to cell A1.

Editing Basics

In this section, we briefly cover some simple ways of revising and manipulating worksheets so that in future chapters we can give general editing instructions without having to go into great detail.

Changing Entries

First let's see how to change individual entries. Glancing down the Amount of Sale column in the INVOICES worksheet, notice that the amount in cell D4 is suspiciously large compared with all other amounts. Suppose you check this number and find to your disappointment that the amount should be 63456.83, not 634568.3. Here's how you correct the entry without having to retype the whole thing:

Direct in-cell editing

1. Double-click cell D4. An insertion point appears at the end of the current entry.

2. In the cell, point between the 6 and 8 and click the left mouse button to position the insertion point. Then type a period (.).

3. Click between the second period and the 3 and press the Backspace key to delete the second period.

4. Press Enter to confirm the corrected entry.

   You can also simply click a cell and make changes in the edit line's contents box.

Copying Entries

You can copy an entry or group of entries anywhere within the same worksheet or in a different worksheet. Copy operations involve the use of two commands: Copy and Paste. You can choose these commands from the Edit menu, or you can click the equivalent icons on the SmartIcon palette. Follow these steps:

1. Select A1..D12 and click the Copy icon or choose Copy from the Edit menu. 1-2-3 stores a copy of the entries in the selected range on the Windows Clipboard.

2. Select cell E1 and click the Paste icon or choose Paste from the Edit menu. 1-2-3 assumes that the selected cell is the top left corner of the paste area and pastes the copied entries into E1..H12. (Notice that you don't have to select the entire paste area.)

Now try using 1-2-3's quick menus:

1. Select cell F1 and then click it with the right mouse button. (From now on, we'll refer to this action as *right-clicking*.) This quick menu pops up:

Displaying quick menus

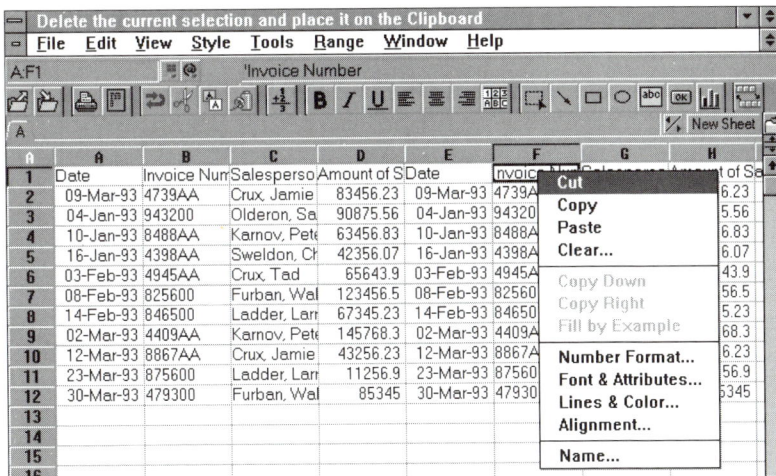

2. Choose Paste from the quick menu. 1-2-3 uses the selected cell as the top left corner of the paste area and, without warning, pastes the copied cells over the existing contents of cells F1..I12, like this:

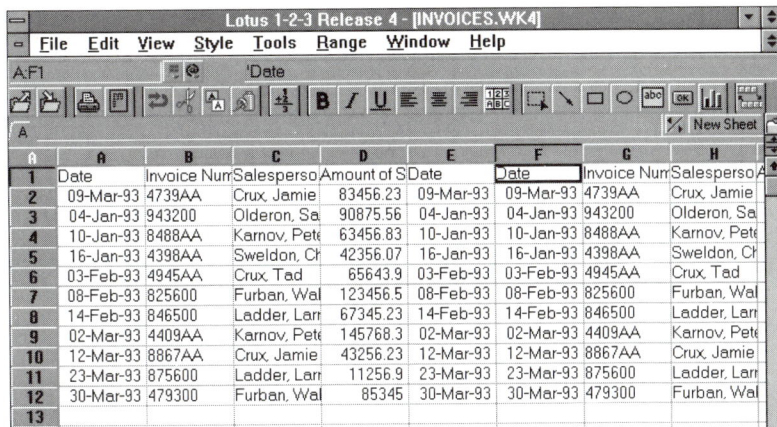

The Clipboard

The Windows Clipboard temporarily stores cut or copied data from all Windows applications. You can also use it to transfer data from the documents of one application to those of another. Each item you cut or copy overwrites the previous item. Because the Clipboard is a temporary storage space, exiting Windows or turning off your computer erases any information that is stored there, unless you save the Clipboard file. You can save the file by switching to Program Manager, double-clicking the Clipboard icon (or the Clipboard Viewer icon) to display the Clipboard window, and then choosing Save As from the File menu.

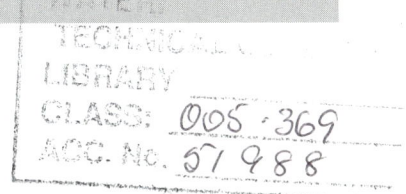

Cause for panic? Not at all. 1-2-3's Undo command is designed for just such an occasion.

Undoing commands

3. Click the Undo icon or choose Undo from the Edit menu. 1-2-3 restores your worksheet to its prepaste status. (If Undo doesn't seem to work, choose User Setup from the Tools menu, select the Undo option, click OK, and try this step again.)

The copied information is still on the Clipboard, so let's make yet another copy, this time in the FILE0001 worksheet:

1. Choose FILE0001.WK4 from the Window menu. If necessary, press the Home key to move the cell pointer to A1.

2. Click the Paste icon. 1-2-3 faithfully pastes in a copy of the range from the INVOICES worksheet.

You can also use a simple mouse operation to copy and paste cells within a single worksheet. Follow these steps:

Drag-and-drop copying

1. Select A1..D12 in FILE0001 and move the pointer over the border of the selected range.

2. When the pointer changes to a hand, hold down the Ctrl key, hold down the left mouse button, and drag until the outline of the selection is over the range E1..H12. While you drag, a plus sign appears in the center of the hand pointer.

3. Release the mouse button and the Ctrl key. 1-2-3 pastes a copy of the selected cells into the designated paste area.

Copying with the Ctrl key

You can use a keyboard shortcut to copy a range to the Windows Clipboard and paste it from the Clipboard into your worksheet. Simply highlight the range and press Ctrl-C. Then move the cell pointer to the top left corner of the destination range and press Ctrl-V.

The outcome of this operation is similar to using the Copy and Paste icons or the equivalent commands, except that 1-2-3 doesn't place a copy of the selected range on the Clipboard. As a result, you can use this technique to copy and paste only within a single worksheet. Because dragging requires that you hold down both the Ctrl key and the mouse button, it's probably best reserved for copying and pasting a small range a short distance from the original.

Moving Entries

The procedure for moving cell entries is almost identical to that for copying entries. Again, you use two commands: Cut and Paste. You can choose these commands from the Edit menu, or you can click the equivalent icons. Try this:

1. Choose Tile from the Window menu to display both open worksheets.

2. Activate INVOICES.WK4 and use the horizontal scroll bar to bring columns E through H into view. Select E1..H12 in INVOICES, and either choose Cut from the Edit menu or right-click the range and choose Cut from its quick menu.

3. Select A13 in FILE0001, and either choose Paste from the Edit menu or right-click A13 and choose Paste from its quick menu. 1-2-3 moves the entries from E1..H12 of INVOICES to A13..D24 of FILE0001, and your worksheets now look like this:

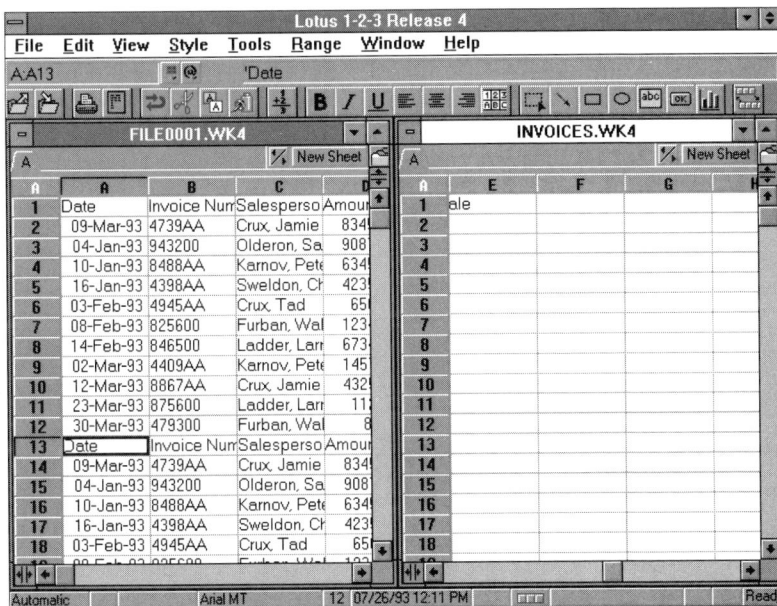

4. For a better view of the results in FILE0001, click the Maximize button at the right end of its title bar.

You can also move entries within a single worksheet by dragging them. Follow these steps:

1. Select A13..D24 in FILE0001 and move the pointer over the border of the selected range.

Drag-and-drop moving

2. When the pointer changes to a hand, hold down the left mouse button, and drag until the outline of the selection is over the range E13..H24. (Notice that you don't hold down the Ctrl key for a move operation.)

3. Release the mouse button. 1-2-3 moves the entries in the selected cells to their new location.

4. Choose the Undo command from the Edit menu to move the entries back to A13..D24.

Inserting and Deleting Cells

It is a rare person who can create a worksheet from scratch without ever having to tinker with its design—moving this block of data, changing that heading, or adding or deleting a column here and there. In this section, we'll show you how to insert cells. Follow these steps:

1. We'll work with the INVOICES worksheet for this section, so choose it from the Window menu and press the Home key to move the cell pointer to cell A1.

Inserting columns

2. Click the column D header—the box containing the letter D—to select the entire column.

3. Choose Insert from either the Edit menu or the column's quick menu. 1-2-3 inserts an entire blank column in front of the Amount of Sale column which, as you can see here, is now column E:

	A	B	C	D	E	F	G	H
1	Date	Invoice Num	Salesperso		Amount of Sale			
2	09-Mar-93	4739AA	Crux, Jamie		83456.23			
3	04-Jan-93	943200	Olderon, Sam		90875.56			
4	10-Jan-93	8488AA	Karnov, Peter		63456.83			
5	16-Jan-93	4398AA	Sweldon, Chaz		42356.07			
6	03-Feb-93	4945AA	Crux, Tad		65643.9			
7	08-Feb-93	825600	Furban, Wally		123456.5			
8	14-Feb-93	846500	Ladder, Larry		67345.23			
9	02-Mar-93	4409AA	Karnov, Peter		145768.3			
10	12-Mar-93	8867AA	Crux, Jamie		43256.23			
11	23-Mar-93	875600	Ladder, Larry		11256.9			
12	30-Mar-93	479300	Furban, Wally		85345			
13								

Inserting a row works exactly the same way as inserting a column. You simply click the row header—the box containing the row number—to select the entire row and choose Insert from either the Edit menu or the row's quick menu.

Inserting rows

What if you need to insert only a few cells and inserting an entire column will mess up some of your entries? You can insert cells anywhere you need them, as you'll see by following these steps:

1. Select E1..E10—all but two of the cells containing entries in column E—and choose Insert from the Edit menu. 1-2-3 displays this dialog box:

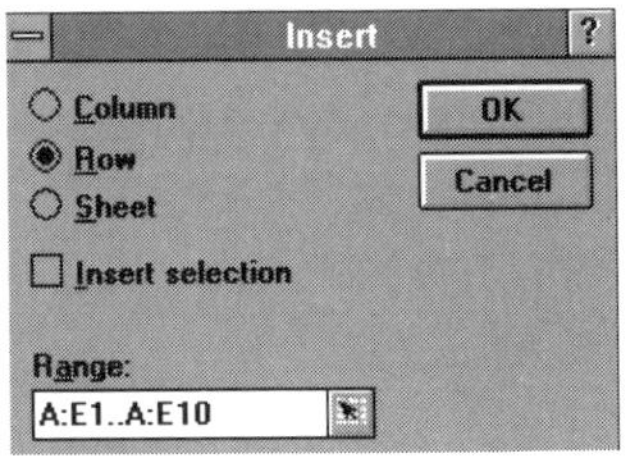

Inserting cells

Because you have selected a range rather than the entire column, 1-2-3 needs to know which cells to move to make room for the inserted cells.

2. Click the Column option to move the existing cells to the column on the right. Then click the Insert Selection box to tell 1-2-3 to insert cells only in the selected range. Finally, click OK. 1-2-3 inserts a new blank cell to the left of each selected cell, as shown here:

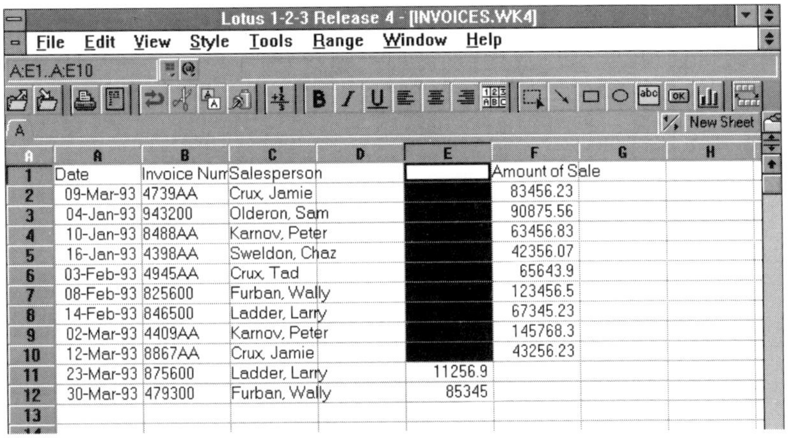

You could undo this insertion to restore the integrity of the Amount of Sale column, but instead let's delete E1..E10:

Deleting cells

1. With E1..E10 selected, choose Delete from the Edit menu. 1-2-3 displays a Delete dialog box similar to the Insert dialog box shown on page 25.

2. Click the Column option and the Delete Selection box to tell 1-2-3 to shift cells to the left to fill the gap left by the deleted cells. Then click OK. 1-2-3 deletes the cells, and the sale amounts are now back in one column.

You can leave the empty column D where it is for now—you'll use it when we work with the INVOICES worksheet again in the next chapter.

Formatting Basics

1-2-3 offers a wide variety of formatting options that allow you to emphasize parts of your worksheet and display data in different ways. Here we'll look at some of the formatting options that are available with the SmartIcons. We'll also show you a quick way to adjust column widths. Later, when you have more 1-2-3 experience, you might want to explore the additional formatting options available on the Style menu.

Changing Character Styles

Just as you can use headings to make tables of data easier to read, you can use styles to distinguish different categories of information. Styles change the appearance of the characters in the worksheet. For example, you might apply the Bold style to major headings and the Bold and Italic styles to minor headings to make them stand out. Because these character styles are used so often, 1-2-3 provides SmartIcons for them. Try this:

1. Select A1..E1, the range that contains the headings.

B

2. Click the Bold icon. The headings are now displayed in bold.

Changing Alignment

As you know, by default 1-2-3 left-aligns labels (text entries) and right-aligns values (numeric entries). You can override the default alignment by using the Alignment SmartIcons. Here's how:

1. With A1..E1 still selected, click each Alignment icon, noting its effect.

2. When you're ready, click the Center icon, which is a typical choice for headings.

Changing Column Widths

As a finishing touch for your first worksheet, you'll want to adjust the widths of columns B, C, and E so that the column headings fit neatly in their cells. Here's what you do:

1. Move the mouse pointer to the dividing line between the headers of columns B and C. The pointer shape changes to a vertical bar with two opposing arrows.

Manual adjustment

2. Hold down the left mouse button and drag to the right until column B is wide enough to display the Invoice Number heading. Release the mouse button when you think that the label will fit in the cell.

3. Change the width of column E using this same method. Move the mouse pointer between the headers of columns E and F. Hold down the mouse button and drag to the right until column E is wide enough to display its heading.

Now we'll widen columns C and D using a different method:

1. Select C1..D1 and choose Column Width from the Style menu. 1-2-3 displays the Column Width dialog box:

Using the Column Width command

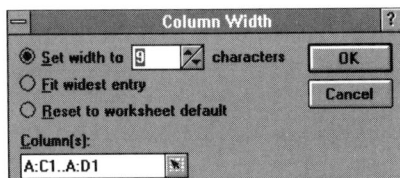

Because you have not adjusted the widths of columns C and D before, 9—the standard width—is displayed in the Set Width To edit box.

2. Click the upward-pointing arrowhead to the right of the edit box until 12 appears in the box. Then click OK. Here's the result:

Lotus 1-2-3 Release 4 - [INVOICES.WK4]

File   Edit   View   Style   Tools   Range   Window   Help

A:C1..A:D1   ^Salesperson

	A	B	C	D	E	F
1	Date	Invoice Number	Salesperson		Amount of Sale	
2	09-Mar-93	4739AA	Crux, Jamie		83456.23	
3	04-Jan-93	943200	Olderon, Sam		90875.56	
4	10-Jan-93	8488AA	Karnov, Peter		63456.83	
5	16-Jan-93	4398AA	Sweldon, Chaz		42356.07	
6	03-Feb-93	4945AA	Crux, Tad		65643.9	
7	08-Feb-93	825600	Furban, Wally		123456.45	
8	14-Feb-93	846500	Ladder, Larry		67345.23	
9	02-Mar-93	4409AA	Karnov, Peter		145768.34	
10	12-Mar-93	8867AA	Crux, Jamie		43256.23	
11	23-Mar-93	875600	Ladder, Larry		11256.9	
12	30-Mar-93	479300	Furban, Wally		85345	
13						

Adjusting row heights

You can adjust the height of rows the same way you adjust the width of columns. Simply drag the bottom header border of the row up or down, or choose Row Height from the Style menu to make the row shorter or taller.

Working with Multiple Sheets

Up to now you have been working with two separate worksheets, one saved under the name INVOICES.WK4 and the other unsaved with the default name FILE0001.WK4. As we mentioned earlier, 1-2-3 also allows you to work with multiple sheets within a single worksheet. The initial sheet in a worksheet is named A, and subsequent sheets are named B, C, D, and so on. In the following examples, you'll add sheets B and C to the FILE0001 worksheet and then copy information to these new sheets.

Perspective view

To see more than one sheet in a window, you toggle the active worksheet into perspective view. Follow these steps:

1. Choose FILE0001.WK4 from the Window menu to make it active.

2. Choose Split from the View menu to display this dialog box:

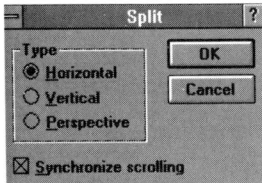

3. Click the Perspective option and then click OK. 1-2-3 closes the dialog box and divides the view of FILE0001 into three sections. As shown here, the bottom section shows sheet A, and the middle and top sections are empty:

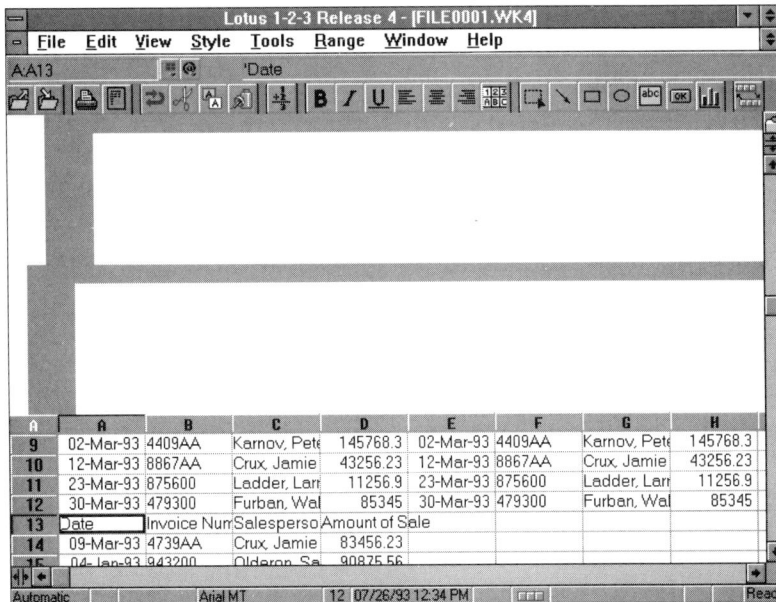

4. Choose Insert from the Edit menu to display the Insert dialog box shown earlier on page 25.

Inserting sheets

5. Click the Sheet option. The Insert Selection option is replaced by Before and After buttons and a Quantity edit box.

6. Click the upward-pointing arrowhead to the right of the Quantity edit box to change the number of sheets to be inserted to 2. Then click OK. As you can see on the next page, 1-2-3 inserts sheets B and C in the FILE0001.WK4 window.

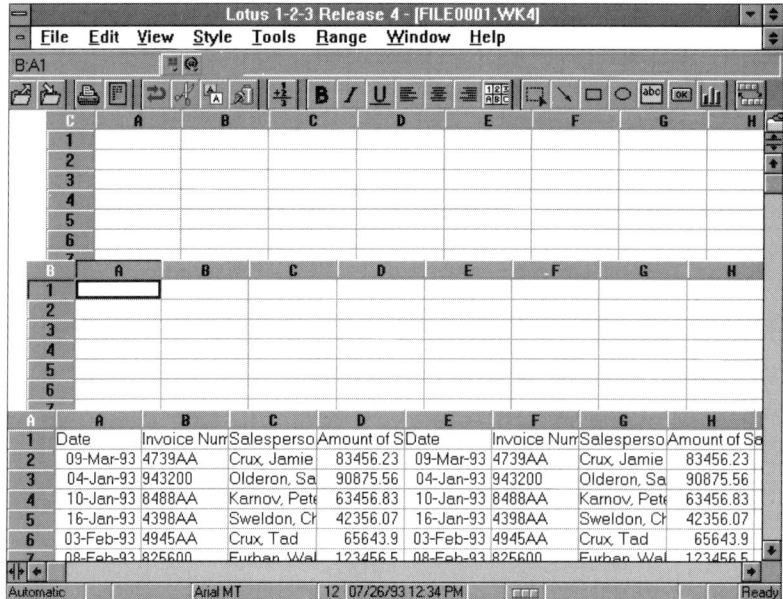

7. In the bottom sheet, select A:A13..A:D24. (When working with multiple sheets, we'll follow 1-2-3's lead and use sheet letters to clearly identify cell selections.)

8. Click the Cut icon to cut the entries from the range.

9. Select B:A1, click the Paste icon, then select C:A1, and click the Paste icon again. Here is the worksheet window after you complete these steps:

Synchronized scrolling

If you split the worksheet window and then use the scroll bars to move around, all views of the worksheet scroll in unison. You can turn off synchronized scrolling by choosing the Split command from the View menu and deselecting the Synchronized Scrolling check box.

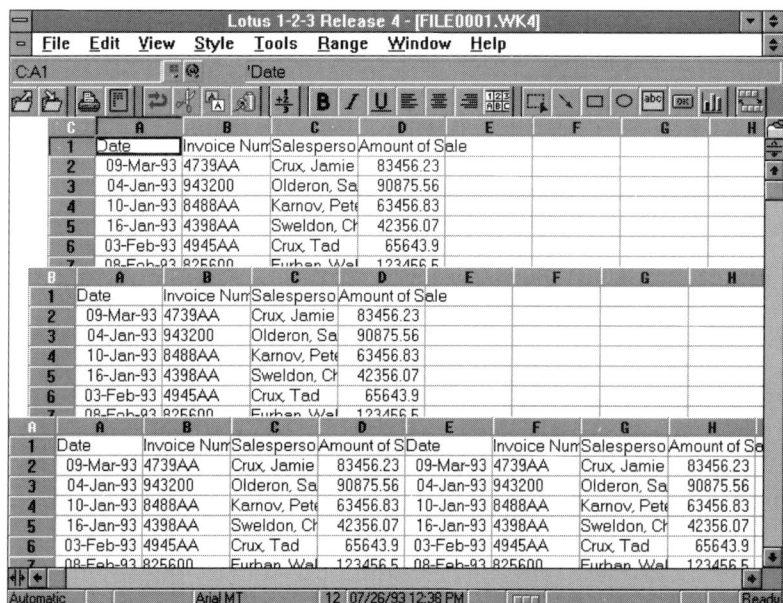

If you were to save FILE0001.WK4 now, 1-2-3 would save all three sheets—A, B, and C—as part of the worksheet file. This capability of handling multiple sheets in a worksheet— also known as *three-dimensional worksheets*—is one of the powerful features of 1-2-3 for Windows. You can take advantage of this feature to organize different but related parts of a worksheet within the context of a single file.

Using Sheet Tabs

You don't have to be content with viewing small portions of the sheets in a worksheet; you can expand them to fill the entire screen. To move between full-screen sheets, you click tabs that resemble those on file folders. Try this:

1. Choose Clear Split from the View menu to return to single-sheet view. Your screen now looks like this:

Single-sheet view

As you can see, 1-2-3 displays tabs for each sheet, and the last sheet you worked with, C, is active. The selection indicator contains the sheet letter and reference of the active cell.

2. Add another sheet to this worksheet by clicking the New Sheet button at the right end of the tab line. 1-2-3 inserts a new sheet after the active sheet.

Adding new sheets

3. Move between the sheets by clicking their tabs, returning to sheet C when you're ready.

Clearing Cells and Deleting Sheets

Now for a couple of other experiments. First, we'll clear some cells. Clearing cells is different from cutting entries. Cutting assumes that you will paste the entries somewhere else, whereas clearing cells simply erases the entries. In the following example, you'll first clear some cells from sheet C, and then you'll delete the entire sheet from the FILE0001 worksheet:

1. Click the C tab, select C:A1..C:D12 and press the Delete or Del key. The entries in the range disappear.

2. With sheet C still active, choose the Delete command from the Edit menu to display the Delete dialog box:

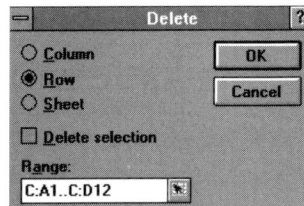

3. Select Sheet and click OK. 1-2-3 deletes sheet C from the FILE0001 worksheet, and sheet D becomes sheet C.

Getting Help

This tour of 1-2-3 has covered a lot of ground in a few pages, and you might be wondering how you will manage to retain it all. Don't worry. If you forget how to carry out a particular task, help is never far away. For example, let's see how you would remind yourself of how to save a worksheet:

Context-sensitive help

1. Pull down the File menu, use the Down Arrow key to highlight the Save command, and press the F1 key to display a Help window with information about the Save command.

2. If necessary, click the Maximize button at the right end of the Help window's title bar. Your screen now looks like this:

```
┌─────────────────────────────────────────────────────────────┐
│ ─                    1-2-3 Release 4 Help          ▼ ◆        │
├─────────────────────────────────────────────────────────────┤
│ File   Edit   Bookmark   Help                                 │
├─────────────────────────────────────────────────────────────┤
│ Contents │ Search │ Back │ History │  <<  │   >>  │           │
├─────────────────────────────────────────────────────────────┤
│ File Save                                                     │
│ File Save Versions                                            │
│ File Update                                                   │
├───────────────────────────────────────────────────────────┬─┤
│ Saves the current worksheet file on disk; saves the current │▲│
│ version of a shared file; updates a 1-2-3                   │ │
│ Worksheet object in another application file.               │ │
│                                                             │ │
│  If the file you save        Then 1-2-3                     │ │
│                                                             │ │
│  Is new                      Lets you enter a file name     │ │
│                              before confirming the save.    │ │
│  Already exists              Updates the contents of the    │ │
│                              file on disk.                  │ │
│  Is a shared file            Changes the command from File  │ │
│                              Save to File Save Versions and │ │
│                              saves new versions and         │ │
│                              scenarios to a Lotus Notes     │ │
│                              server. See Sharing Files      │ │
│                              Using Lotus Notes before you   │ │
│                              use File Save Versions.        │ │
│  Is a 1-2-3 Worksheet object Changes the command from File  │ │
│                              Save to File Update and        │ │
│                              updates the                    │ │
│                              1-2-3 Worksheet object         │ │
│                              embedded in another            │ │
│                              application file.              │ │
│                                                             │ │
│  1.  Make sure the cell pointer is in the file you want to  │ │
│      save.                                                  │ │
│  2.  Choose File Save, File Save Versions, or File Update.  │ │
│      If the file is new, specify the name of the file in    │ │
│      the File Save As dialog box.                           │ │
│  Note File Save saves worksheet data and associated styles  │ │
│  in a single file with the extension .WK4,                  │▼│
│  unless the file already has another file extension.        │ │
└───────────────────────────────────────────────────────────┴─┘
```

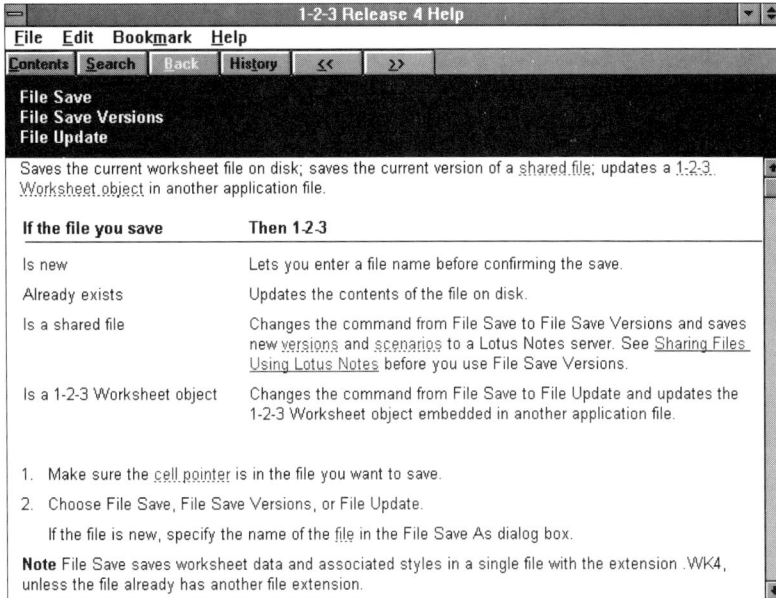

3. Click the Contents button below the menu bar to display a list of general topics that provide information about 1-2-3.

General Help topics

4. Choose How To Use Help from the Help menu and scroll through the information, exploring the various aspects of 1-2-3's Help system. (Clicking words with dotted underscores displays pop-up definitions of terms, and clicking topics with solid underscores takes you to those topics. Clicking the Back button allows you to trace your way back to the How To Use Help contents window.)

Learning to use Help

5. When you are ready, choose Exit from the File menu to close the Help window and return to your worksheet.

Quitting 1-2-3

Well, that's it for the basic tour. All that's left is to show you how to end a 1-2-3 session. Follow these steps:

1. Choose Exit from the File menu.

2. When 1-2-3 asks if you want to save the changes you have made to the open worksheets, click No for FILE0001.WK4 and click Yes for INVOICE.WK4.

2

Analyzing Information

What you will learn

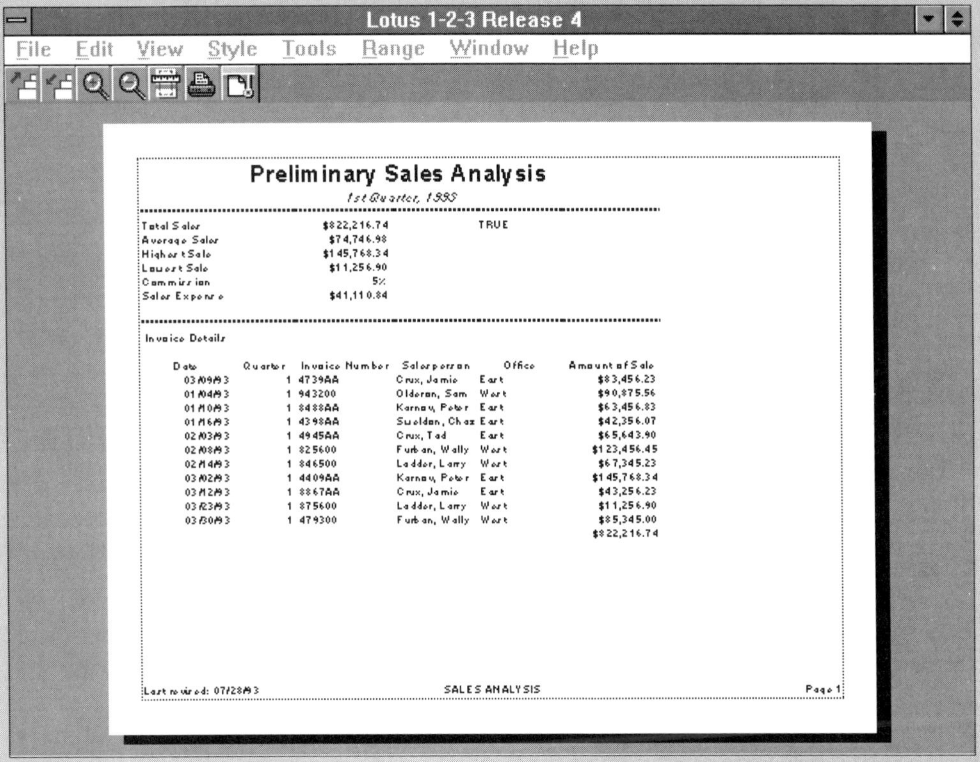

Lotus 1-2-3 Release 4
File Edit View Style Tools Range Window Help
Preliminary Sales Analysis
1st Quarter, 1993
Total Sales $822,216.74 TRUE
Average Sales $74,746.98
Highest Sale $145,768.34
Lowest Sale $11,256.90
Commission 5%
Sales Expense $41,110.84
Invoice Details
Date Quarter Invoice Number Salesperson Office Amount of Sale
03/09/93 1 4739AA Crux, Jamie East $83,456.23
01/04/93 1 943200 Olderan, Sam West $90,875.56
01/10/93 1 8488AA Karnay, Peter East $63,456.83
01/16/93 1 4398AA Sweldon, Chaz East $42,356.07
02/03/93 1 4945AA Crux, Tad East $65,643.90
02/08/93 1 825600 Furban, Wally West $123,456.45
02/14/93 1 846500 Ladder, Larry West $67,345.23
03/02/93 1 4409AA Karnay, Peter East $145,768.34
03/12/93 1 8867AA Crux, Jamie East $43,256.23
03/23/93 1 875600 Ladder, Larry West $11,256.90
03/30/93 1 479300 Furban, Wally West $85,345.00
$822,216.74
Last revised: 07/28/93
SALES ANALYSIS
Page 1

C hapter 1 covered some 1-2-3 basics, and you now know enough to create simple tables. But you are missing the essential piece of information that turns a table into a worksheet: how to enter formulas. The whole purpose of building worksheets is to have 1-2-3 perform calculations for you. In this chapter, we show you how to retrieve the INVOICES worksheet and enter formulas to analyze sales. (If you don't work in sales, you can adapt the worksheet to analyze other sources of income such as service fees or subscriptions.) Along the way, we cover some powerful techniques for manipulating data and a few principles of worksheet design. Finally, we spell-check and print the INVOICES worksheet. So fire up 1-2-3, and we'll get started.

Opening Existing Worksheets

When you first start 1-2-3, the worksheet window contains a blank document named Untitled. You can open a worksheet you have already created using several methods. If the worksheet is one of the last five you have worked with, you can simply choose the file from the bottom of the File menu. Otherwise, you can use the Open command on the File menu or the Open icon on the SmartIcon palette to retrieve the worksheet. We'll use the first method:

Opening worksheets

1. Choose INVOICE.WK4 from the bottom of the File menu. 1-2-3 displays the table you created in Chapter 1.

Simple Calculations

1-2-3 has many powerful functions that are a sort of shorthand for the various formulas used in mathematical, logical, statistical, financial, trigonometric, logarithmic, and other types of calculations. However, the majority of worksheets created with 1-2-3 involve simple arithmetic. In this section, we show you how to use the four arithmetic operators (+, −, *, and /) to add, subtract, multiply, and divide, and then we introduce two 1-2-3 features with which you can quickly add sets of numeric values.

Doing Arithmetic

You begin a formula with a digit or a special character, such as +, that toggles 1-2-3 into Value mode. The simplest formulas contain values separated by +, −, *, or /, such as

5+3+2

If you enter this formula in any blank cell in your worksheet, 1-2-3 displays the result 10.

Let's experiment with a few formulas. We'll start by inserting a couple of blank rows:

1. Click the header for row 1 and drag down through the header for row 2 to select the two rows.

Inserting multiple rows

2. Right-click anywhere in the selected rows and choose Insert from the quick menu. Because you selected two rows, 1-2-3 inserts two blank rows above the table, moving the table down so that it begins in row 3.

Now we're ready to construct a formula in cell A1, using some of the values in the Amount of Sale column. You tell 1-2-3 to use a value simply by clicking the cell that contains it. Follow these steps:

1. With cell A1 active, type an opening parenthesis. The mode indicator displays the word Value to indicate the beginning of a formula.

2. Click cell E4. 1-2-3 inserts the cell reference E4 in the cell and the contents box.

3. Type a plus sign, and click cell E5. 1-2-3 adds the cell reference E5 to the formula.

4. Continue to build the formula by typing plus signs and clicking cells E6, E7, and E8.

5. Type a closing parenthesis followed by a / (the division operator), and then type 5. The formula now looks like the one on the next page.

This formula tells 1-2-3 to first add the amounts in cells E4, E5, E6, E7, and E8 and then divide the result by 5, to obtain the average of the five amounts.

6. Click the Confirm button. 1-2-3 displays the result of the formula, 69157.72, in cell A1.

You can use this technique to create any simple formula. You start by typing a plus sign, an open parenthesis, and a digit or some other character that signals the beginning of a formula. Then you type a value or click the cell that contains the value, type the appropriate arithmetic operator, enter the next value, and so on. 1-2-3 performs multiplication and division before addition and subtraction. If you need parts of the formula to be carried out in a specific order, use parentheses as we did in the previous calculation to override the default order.

Order of precedence

Totaling Columns of Values

Although this method of creating a formula is simple enough, it would be tedious to have to type and click to add a long series of values. Fortunately, 1-2-3 automates the addition process with a very useful tool: the Sum icon.

Using the Sum Icon

The Sum icon will probably become one of your most often-used 1-2-3 tools. In fact, using this tool is so easy that we'll dispense with explanations and simply show you what to do:

1. Move the cell pointer to E15.

2. Click the Sum icon in the SmartIcon palette. 1-2-3 looks above and to the left of the active cell for the largest range of values to total. Because there are no values to the left of E15, 1-2-3 assumes that you want to total the values above it. 1-2-3 enters an @SUM function in cell E15 and the contents box and displays the result of the function, 822216.74—the total of the range E4..E14. Your worksheet looks like this:

	A	B	C	D	E	F
1	69157.72					
2						
3	Date	Invoice Number	Salesperson		Amount of Sale	
4	09-Mar-93	4739AA	Crux, Jamie		83456.23	
5	04-Jan-93	943200	Olderon, Sam		90875.56	
6	10-Jan-93	8488AA	Karnov, Peter		63456.83	
7	16-Jan-93	4398AA	Sweldon, Chaz		42356.07	
8	03-Feb-93	4945AA	Crux, Tad		65643.9	
9	08-Feb-93	825600	Furban, Wally		123456.45	
10	14-Feb-93	846500	Ladder, Larry		67345.23	
11	02-Mar-93	4409AA	Karnov, Peter		145768.34	
12	12-Mar-93	8867AA	Crux, Jamie		43256.23	
13	23-Mar-93	875600	Ladder, Larry		11256.9	
14	30-Mar-93	479300	Furban, Wally		85345	
15					822216.74	
16						

That was easy. The Sum icon will serve you well whenever you want a total to appear at the bottom of a column or to the right of a row of values. But what if you want the total to appear elsewhere on the worksheet? Knowing how to create @SUM functions from scratch gives you more flexibility.

Using the @SUM Function

Let's go back and dissect the @SUM function that 1-2-3 inserted in cell E15 when you clicked the Sum icon so that you can examine the function's components.

With the cell pointer still at E15, you can see the following entry in the contents box:

@SUM(E4..E14)

Like all function names in 1-2-3, @SUM begins with an "at" symbol (@). If you are entering this function directly from the keyboard, the @ symbol switches 1-2-3 into Value mode. Next comes the function name in capital letters, followed by a set of parentheses enclosing the reference of the range

Function names

When you type a function name, such as @SUM, in the contents box, you don't have to type it in capital letters. 1-2-3 capitalizes the function name for you when you complete the entry. If 1-2-3 does not respond in this way, you have probably entered the function name incorrectly.

Arguments

containing the amounts you want to total. This reference is the @SUM function's *argument*. An argument answers questions such as "What?" or "How?" and gives 1-2-3 the additional information it needs to perform the function. In the case of @SUM, 1-2-3 needs only one piece of information—the references of the cells you want to total. As you'll see later, 1-2-3 might need several pieces of information to carry out other functions, and you enter an argument for each piece.

Creating an @SUM formula from scratch is not particularly difficult. For practice, follow these steps:

1. Press the Home key to move to cell A1, and type this:

@SUM(

When you begin typing, the cell's old value is overwritten.

2. Select E4..E14 on the worksheet in the usual way. 1-2-3 inserts the reference E4..E14 after the opening parenthesis.

3. Type a closing parenthesis and press Enter. 1-2-3 displays in cell A1 the total of the values in the Amount of Sale column— 822216.7. Because the widths of cells A1 and E15 are different, their displayed results are slightly different, but their underlying values are identical.

Referencing Cells Containing Formulas in Other Formulas

After you create a formula in one cell, you can use its result in other formulas simply by referencing its cell. To see how this works, follow these steps:

1. Select cell B1 and type a plus sign.

2. Click cell A1, which contains the @SUM function you just entered, type a / (the division operator), and then type *11*.

3. Press Enter. 1-2-3 displays the result—the average of the invoice amounts—in cell B1.

4. Press the Delete key to erase both the experimental formula and its result from cell B1. We discuss an easier way to calculate averages on page 52.

Displaying formulas

By default, 1-2-3 displays the results of formulas rather than the underlying formulas themselves. To see the actual formulas in a worksheet, choose Worksheet Defaults from the Style menu, select Text from the Format list box, and click OK. After you have viewed the formulas on your worksheet, you can quickly restore the display of results by clicking the Undo icon on the SmartIcon palette.

Naming Cells and Ranges

Many of the calculations that you might want to perform on this worksheet—for example, calculating each invoice amount as a percentage of total sales—will use the total you have calculated in cell A1. You could include a copy of the @SUM function now in cell A1 in these other calculations, or you could simply reference cell A1.

The latter method seems quick and simple, but what if you subsequently move the formula in A1 to another location. 1-2-3 gives you a way to reference this formula, no matter where on the worksheet you move it. You can assign A1 a name and then use the name in any calculations that involve the total.

You assign a name to a cell by choosing Name from the Range menu. Follow these steps:

1. Select cell A1 and choose Name from the Range menu. 1-2-3 displays the Name dialog box:

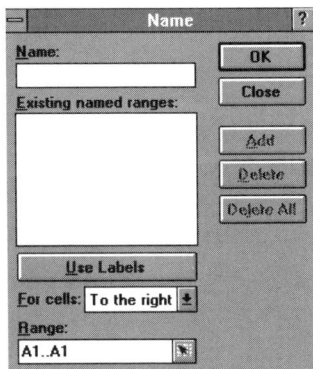

Assigning cell names

As you can see, the reference A1..A1 is displayed in the Range edit box.

2. Type *total* in the Name edit box. (You can enter this name in any combination of uppercase or lowercase letters, and 1-2-3 will convert it to all uppercase letters.)

3. Click OK to assign the name TOTAL to the contents of A1.

To see how 1-2-3 uses the names you assign, follow the steps on the next page.

Range-name conventions

Some rules apply when you name cells or ranges. Names can contain up to 15 characters. 1-2-3 recommends against starting a name with a number. You can use letters, numbers, and underscore characters in any combination of uppercase or lowercase. Do not begin a name with an exclamation point (!). For readability, you might want to use underscore characters in place of spaces. For example, you might define a name as TOTALS_1993.

1. Click cell E15, which currently contains the @SUM function you inserted earlier in the chapter.

2. Type +*total* and press Enter. The worksheet does not appear to change, but now instead of two @SUM functions, the worksheet contains only one. You have told 1-2-3 to assign the value of the cell named TOTAL, which contains the @SUM function, to cell E15.

Assigning range names

You can also assign names to ranges. Let's assign the name AMOUNT to the cells containing amounts in column E:

1. Select E4..E14 and choose Name from the Range menu.

2. Type *amount* in the Name edit box and click OK.

3. Interestingly, 1-2-3 automatically replaces the range reference in the @SUM function in cell A1 with the range name you just created. To see the name, press the Home key to move the cell pointer to cell A1 and look at the contents box. The entry in A1 is now the formula @SUM(AMOUNT).

1-2-3 provides a simple technique for inserting range names in new formulas. While you are entering a formula, you can click the navigator located next to the selection indicator to display a list of all the existing range names. Simply select a name from this list, and 1-2-3 inserts the name in your formula. As an example, follow these steps to reenter the @SUM formula in cell A1:

1. With cell A1 still selected, type @*SUM(*.

2. Click the navigator to display a list of the two names you have defined so far for your worksheet:

Jumping to named cells

To move the cell pointer quickly to a named cell, press the F5 key. 1-2-3 displays the Go To dialog box. Highlight the name of the cell you want to move to, and click OK.

3. Select the name AMOUNT to add it to your formula. The formula in the contents box is now @SUM(AMOUNT.

4. Type a closing parenthesis to complete the formula, and then press Enter. The total in cell A1 remains the same as before.

5. Click the Save icon to save your work.

Quick save

From now on, we won't give you specific instructions to save your work, but you should get in the habit of saving often, perhaps after working through the examples in each section.

Efficient Data Display

Before we discuss other calculations you might want to perform with this worksheet, let's look at ways to format your information to make it easier to read. We'll show you how to make the results of your calculations stand out from your data and how to format the data itself so that it is neat and consistent. As your worksheets grow in complexity, you'll find that paying attention to such details will keep you oriented and help others understand your results.

Creating a Calculation Area

Usually when you create a worksheet, you are interested not so much in the individual pieces of information as in the results of the calculations you perform on the pieces. The current worksheet fits neatly on one screen, but often worksheets of this type include several screenfuls of information. It's a good idea to design your worksheets so that the important information is easily accessible and in a predictable location. For these reasons, we leave room in the top left corner of our worksheets for a calculation area. This habit is useful for the following reasons:

- We don't have to scroll around looking for totals and other results.

- We can print just the first page of the worksheet to get a report of the most pertinent information.

- We can easily jump to the calculation area from anywhere on the worksheet by pressing the Home key to move to cell A1.

Let's create an area at the top of the INVOICES worksheet for a title and a set of calculations. We'll start by freeing up some space at the top of the worksheet:

Moving a range

1. Select A1..E15, use the Cut and Paste commands or drag-and-drop editing to move the selection to A10..E24, and press Home. Your screen now looks like this:

If A10..E24 had contained any data, 1-2-3 would have overwritten it.

Now let's enter a title for the worksheet:

1. In cell A1, type *Preliminary Sales Analysis* and press the Down Arrow key.

2. In cell A2, type *1st Quarter, 1993* and press Enter.

Next, we'll set off the calculation area. With 1-2-3, you can use borders and shading to draw attention to calculation results, and in Chapter 6 we will show you some special techniques for formatting your worksheets. For now, though, let's simply draw lines of asterisks above and below the area. You use a special prefix, the backslash character (\\), to tell 1-2-3 to fill a cell with a character or sequence of characters.

Moving formulas

The formula now in cell A10 remains correct, even though you have moved it from cell A1. How can you move a formula without disturbing the results? The reference in the formula is relative, meaning that it identifies cells according to their relationship to the formula cell. See page 59 for more information.

Here's how to use this prefix, along with the Range Fill icon, to draw a line of asterisks:

1. Select cell A3, type * (a backslash followed by a single asterisk), and press Enter. 1-2-3 fills the cell with asterisks.

2. Select A3..E3 and click the Range Fill icon. 1-2-3 follows the entry pattern in cell A3 and fills the range with asterisks.

3. With A3..E3 still selected, click the Copy icon.

4. Select cell A9 and click the Paste icon to create a line of asterisks at the bottom of the calculation area.

Now that we have created a calculation area, let's move the calculation in cell A10. Follow these steps:

1. Select cell A4, type *Total Sales*, and press Enter.

2. Select cell A10 and use the Cut and Paste commands or drag-and-drop editing to move the formula to cell B4. Here's the result:

Repeating characters

Repeating a pattern

Moving a formula

	A	B	C	D	E	F
1	Preliminary Sales Analysis					
2	1st Quarter, 1993					
3						
4	Total Sales	822216.74				
5						
6						
7						
8						
9						
10						
11						
12	Date	Invoice Number	Salesperson		Amount of Sale	
13	09-Mar-93	4739AA	Crux, Jamie		83456.23	
14	04-Jan-93	943200	Olderon, Sam		90875.56	
15	10-Jan-93	8488AA	Karnov, Peter		63456.83	
16	16-Jan-93	4398AA	Sweldon, Chaz		42356.07	
17	03-Feb-93	4945AA	Crux, Tad		65643.9	
18	08-Feb-93	825600	Furban, Wally		123456.45	
19	14-Feb-93	846500	Ladder, Larry		67345.23	
20	02-Mar-93	4409AA	Karnov, Peter		145768.34	

Flexible repeating characters

You can use the backslash prefix to repeat any character or group of characters so that they fill a cell. Some common examples of repeating characters are hyphens and equal signs. You might also want to experiment with other combinations, such as hyphen-space-asterisk, to create different effects. Using the backslash prefix is more efficient than typing countless characters, not only because it saves typing time but also because it responds to changes you make to column widths. For example, if you decrease the width of column A, 1-2-3 simply adjusts the number of asterisks accordingly.

Formatting Text

In Chapter 1, you learned how to format text in simple ways—using SmartIcons to change alignment and make text bold. In this section, we'll get a bit more elaborate. First let's make the worksheet's title larger so that it really stands out:

The Formatting SmartIcon palette

1. Click the SmartIcon selector in the status bar and choose Formatting to display this Formatting SmartIcon palette, which includes several icons that will be useful in this section:

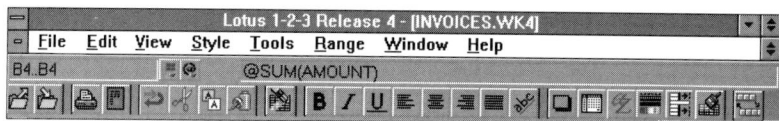

Changing fonts and sizes

2. Select cell A1 and click the Font & Attributes icon. 1-2-3 displays this dialog box:

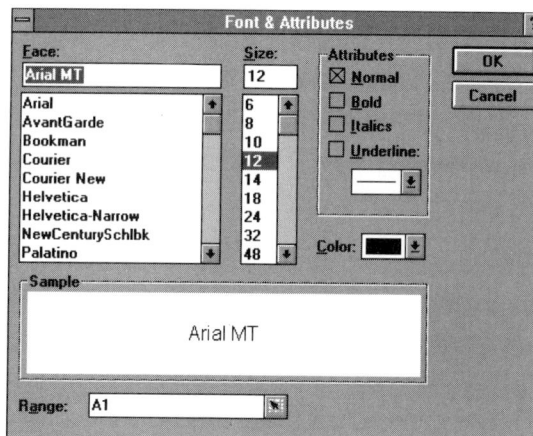

3. Select 24 in the Size list box, click the Bold check box, and then click OK. Notice that the height of row 1 increases to accommodate the larger font.

4. Select cell A2 and click the Font & Attribute icon.

5. Select 14 in the Size list box, click both the Bold and Italics check boxes, and click OK.

Now let's center the text above the calculation area:

Centering across cells

1. Select A1..E2 and choose Alignment from the Style menu to display this dialog box:

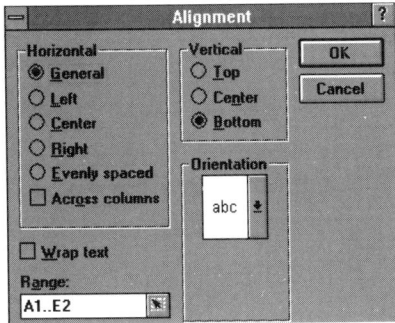

2. In the Horizontal area, click both the Center button and the Across Columns check box, and then click OK.

Now let's add another touch:

1. Select A4..A8, and click the Bold icon on the SmartIcon palette.

2. Click the Fit Widest Entry icon to widen column A so that the Total Sales label fits within the column. From now on, adjust the column widths as necessary to see your work.

Fitting columns to entries

Why did we tell you to select the empty cells below the Total Sales label before applying the Bold format? Try this:

1. Select cell A5, type *Average Sales*, and press Enter. The new label is bold because we already applied the Bold format to cell A5.

2. Click the Fit Widest Entry icon and then press the Home key. Here's the result of your formatting:

Preformatting for efficiency

Formatting blank cells is an efficient way to build a worksheet. For example, if you know that a block of cells will contain the dollar-value result of a formula, you can preformat the entire block.

Displaying Dollars and Cents

With the exception of the date values in column A, 1-2-3 has displayed the values you've entered so far in its default Automatic format. With this format, 1-2-3 simply displays what you typed (or what it thinks you typed). For example, when you entered the dates in Chapter 1, 1-2-3 displayed them in a date format. However, 1-2-3 provides several formats that you can use to change the way the values look. Try this:

1. Select cell E13 and choose Number Format from the Style menu or the cell's quick menu. 1-2-3 displays this dialog box:

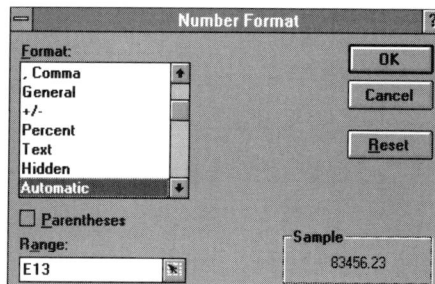

In the Format list box, 1-2-3 highlights Automatic—the default setting. In the bottom right corner, a Sample box shows you how the value in E13 is displayed with the selected format. The following table describes the most frequently used formats:

Format	Effect
Currency	Adds a dollar sign in front of the value, uses commas to group the digits by threes, and displays two decimal places (cents)
Comma	Inserts commas to group the digits in values greater than 999 into threes
Percent	Displays the value as a percentage and appends a percent sign

2. Press the C key. 1-2-3 scrolls the Format list box, highlights Currency (the first format name that starts with the letter *C*), and displays a Decimal Places edit box.

3. Click OK to accept the default setting of 2 decimal places and close the dialog box.

Entering in format

The default number format, Automatic, formats values the way you enter them. For example, entering $123,456.78 applies the Currency format to the current cell. An entry of 12-Dec-93 applies a date format to the current cell. Notice that the number format selector on the status bar changes to reflect any change in the format of the current cell.

Notice that the number format selector at the left end of the status bar has changed from Automatic to Currency to reflect the format of the selected cell. You can save time by applying number formats using this selector. Here's how:

The number format selector

1. Select B4..B8 and click Automatic on the status bar. A menu appears listing the same format options as those in the Number Format dialog box:

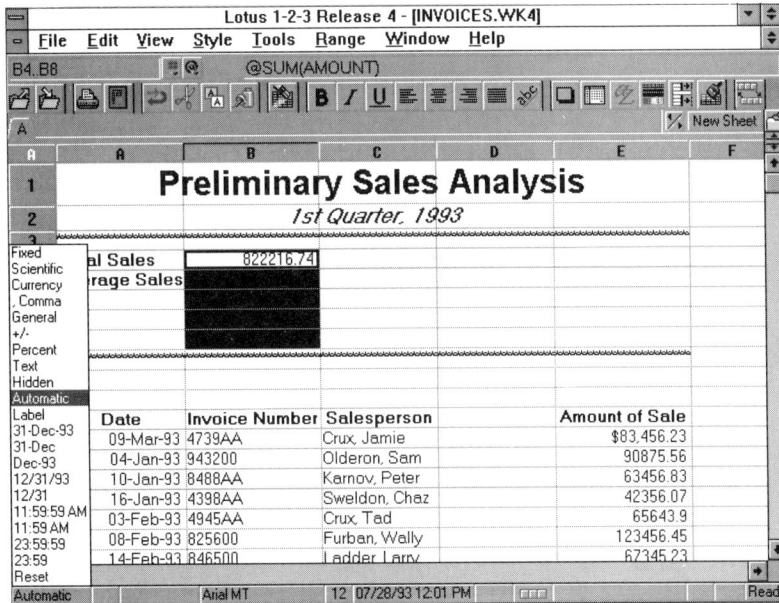

2. Click Currency. 1-2-3 formats the selected cells and changes the number format selector to reflect the new format.

3. To see 1-2-3's default format for negative dollar values, select cell B5, type *–1234*, and click the Down Arrow key. Here's the result:

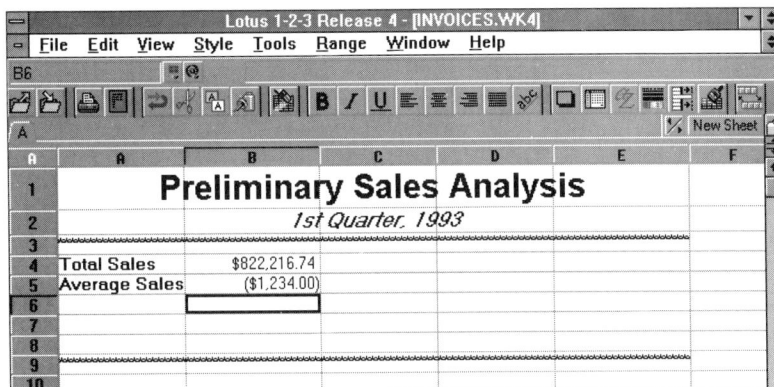

Underlying vs. displayed

After you apply a format, the value displayed in the cell might look different from the value in the contents box. For example, 345.6789 is displayed in its cell as $345.68 if you apply the Currency format. When performing calculations, 1-2-3 will use the value in the contents box, not the displayed value.

As you can see, 1-2-3 displays the negative value in parentheses, aligning the value with the positive value above it and adding a dollar sign, a comma to separate hundreds from thousands, and two zeros to the right of the decimal point.

Formatting Decimal Places

When Currency appears in the number format selector, 1-2-3 displays 2 in the adjacent box to indicate that the default number of decimal places for the Currency format is 2. Whenever a number appears in this box, which is called the *decimal places selector*, you can change the number of decimal places simply by clicking the selector and choosing a new number from the list. Try this:

The decimal places selector

1. Select B4..B5, click the decimal places selector, and choose 0 from the list. 1-2-3 rounds the values in the selected cells to whole dollars.

2. Click the Undo icon to restore the 2 decimal places format.

Formatting Dates

In Chapter 1, we entered dates in column A and then applied a date format to them. 1-2-3's date formats are grouped with its time formats in the Number Format dialog box. Let's experiment with the dates you entered earlier in column A:

1. Select A13..A23 and click the number format selector. In the menu, 1-2-3 highlights the format for the active cell.

2. Select the 31-Dec format and click OK.

3. Experiment with the other date formats to see their effects and then select 12/31/93.

Copying Styles and Formats

In 1-2-3, you can save a lot of formatting time by copying combinations of styles and formats from one cell to other cells. For example, if you format your headings to be bold and centered, you can apply those styles to any cells in the worksheet simply by copying them. Let's give it a try:

1. Select cell A10, type *Invoice Details*, and press Enter.

Changing the format of negative amounts

If you want to display negative dollar values with a minus sign instead of parentheses, choose User Setup from the Tools menu, click the International button, select the Sign option from the Negative Values list, and click OK.

2. Select cell A12, which contains a heading that is bold and centered, and click the Copy Styles icon.

3. Move the pointer, which now has the shape of a paintbrush, to cell A10 and click. 1-2-3 immediately applies both the bold and centered styles to the selected cell.

Now let's format the remaining values in the Amount of Sale column as currency, this time copying the format from cell E13:

1. Select cell E13 and click the Copy Styles icon.

2. Select E14..E24. When you release the mouse button, 1-2-3 applies the Currency format from cell E13 to the selected range, adding dollar signs, commas, and two decimal places to the values. Your worksheet now looks like this:

	A	B	C	D	E	F
4	Total Sales	$822,216.74				
5	Average Sales	($1,234.00)				
6						
7						
8						
9						
10	Invoice Details					
11						
12	Date	Invoice Number	Salesperson		Amount of Sale	
13	03/09/93	4739AA	Crux, Jamie		$83,456.23	
14	01/04/93	943200	Olderon, Sam		$90,875.56	
15	01/10/93	8488AA	Karnov, Peter		$63,456.83	
16	01/16/93	4398AA	Sweldon, Chaz		$42,356.07	
17	02/03/93	4945AA	Crux, Tad		$65,643.90	
18	02/08/93	825600	Furban, Wally		$123,456.45	
19	02/14/93	846500	Ladder, Larry		$67,345.23	
20	03/02/93	4409AA	Karnov, Peter		$145,768.34	
21	03/12/93	8867AA	Crux, Jamie		$43,256.23	
22	03/23/93	875600	Ladder, Larry		$11,256.90	
23	03/30/93	479300	Furban, Wally		$85,345.00	

Named styles

Another easy way to apply combinations of formatting is to create named styles. We discuss this technique on page 133.

From this simple example, you can see how easy it is to build complex combinations of formatting that you can apply with a couple of clicks of the mouse button.

More Calculations

Now let's return to the calculation area and perform some more calculations on the sales data, starting with the average sales.

Averaging Values

To find the average amount for the invoices we've entered in this worksheet, we'll use 1-2-3's @AVG function. We'll use the @function selector on the edit line to avoid making errors while typing function names and to make sure we include all the arguments 1-2-3 needs to calculate the function.

Pasting functions from a list

1. Select cell B5, and click the @function selector. 1-2-3 displays this list of the most frequently used functions:

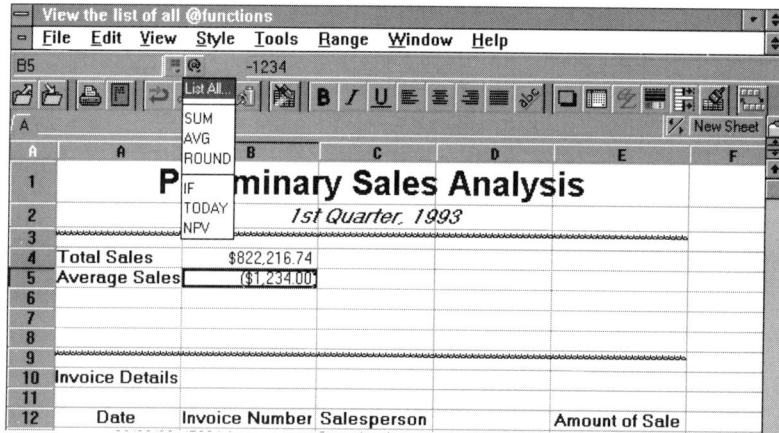

2. Click AVG. 1-2-3 pastes the function with its argument name in the selected cell, which now looks like this:

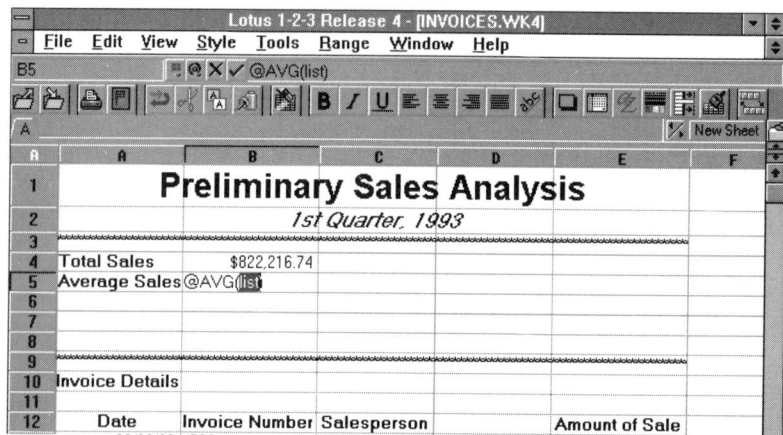

The *list* argument name is highlighted. To calculate the average of a series of values, you could type the values in place of the argument name. In this example, the argument is the reference of the range containing the values to average.

Operators

Here is a list of operators you can use with the @IF function:

= < > <> >= <=

You can also use #AND#, #OR#, and #NOT#. For example, the following formula

@IF(B1=1#AND#C1>1,"Oh","No")

displays Yes only if both conditions are true. This formula

@IF(B1=0#OR#C1>0,"Oh","No")

displays Yes if either condition is true.

3. Select E13..E23 and scroll until the top of the worksheet is back in view. The range reference has replaced *list*, and the cell now looks like this:

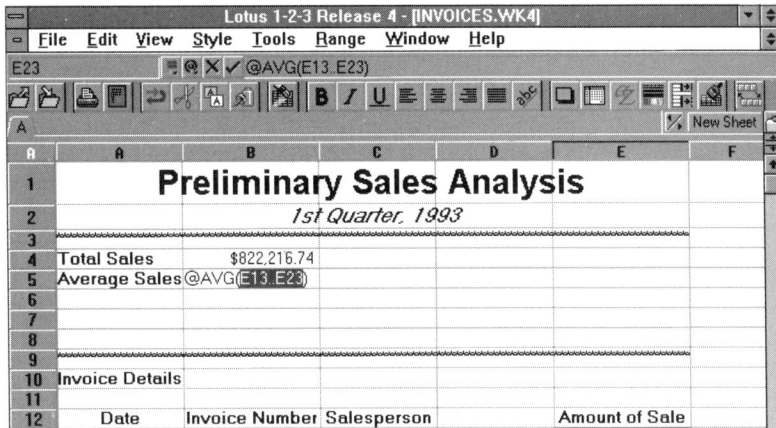

4. Click the Confirm button to enter the formula in cell B5. 1-2-3 displays the result: $74,746.98.

Identifying Highest and Lowest Sales

1-2-3 provides two functions that instantly identify the highest and lowest values in a group. To understand the benefits of these functions, imagine that the INVOICES worksheet contains data from not 11 but 111 invoices! Let's start with the highest sale:

1. Select cell A6, type *Highest Sale*, and press the Right Arrow key to confirm the entry and select cell B6.

2. Click the @function selector and then click the List All option. 1-2-3 displays this dialog box, which lists all the 1-2-3 functions:

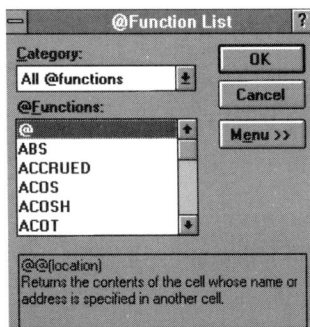

Text values as arguments

When entering text values as arguments in a function or formula, you must enclose them in quotation marks. Otherwise, 1-2-3 thinks the text is a range name. For example,

@RIGHT("Lotus",2)

gives the value "us," but

@RIGHT(Lotus,2)

results in an error—unless the range name LOTUS happens to be defined on the worksheet.

3. Press the M key to bring the function names that begin with the letter *M* into view. Then press Down Arrow to highlight MAX and click OK. 1-2-3 pastes the function with its argument name in the selected cell.

4. Select E13..E23 on the worksheet to replace the argument name with the range reference and then click the Confirm button. 1-2-3 enters the highest sale amount, $145,768.34, in cell B6.

Now for the formula for the lowest sale, which we'll type from scratch:

1. Select cell A7, type *Lowest Sale*, and press Right Arrow key.

2. Type *@MIN(E13..E23)* and press Enter. 1-2-3 displays the result, $11,256.90, in cell B7.

Calculating with Names

The last calculation we'll make with this set of data involves the Total Sales value from cell B4. As a gross indicator of sales expenses, let's calculate the total sales commission:

1. First insert a couple of new rows in the calculation area by clicking the headers for rows 8 and 9 and choosing Insert from the Edit menu or the row quick menu.

2. In cell A8, type *Commission*, and press Right Arrow.

Formatting percentages → **3.** Type *6%* and press Enter. 1-2-3 displays $0.06 because the cell has the currency format.

4. Choose Number Format from the Style menu and click Percent in the Format list box. Then click the down arrow to the right of the Decimal Places edit box twice to change the setting to 0 (zero), and click OK. 1-2-3 now displays the value in B8 as 6%.

We want to assign the label Commission in cell A8 as the name of the value in cell B8. We could assign the name as we did earlier in the chapter (see page 41), but we'll show you an easier way:

1. Press the Left Arrow key to move to A8. Choose Name from the Range menu and click the Use Labels button. 1-2-3 adds the label to the names in the Existing Named Ranges list box.

Assigning labels as range names

2. In the For Cells edit box, 1-2-3 displays To The Right as the default selection for the direction in which the label name will be assigned. Click OK to assign the label in the selected cell to the cell on the right. Though you can't see any difference, cell B8 now has the name COMMISSION.

Now for the formula that will calculate the commission:

1. Select cell A9, type *Sales Expense*, and press Right Arrow.

2. With cell B9 selected, type the formula +*total*commission* and press Enter. 1-2-3 multiplies the value in the cell named TOTAL (B4) by the value in the cell named COMMISSION (B8) and displays the result, $49,333.00, in cell B9. (Notice that 1-2-3 displays the result of the formula in the Currency format. When you inserted two rows earlier, those rows assumed the formatting of the selected rows.)

3. Now select cell B8, type *5%*, and press Enter. Instantly, the value in cell B9 changes to reflect the new commission rate, as shown here:

If a hundred calculations throughout the worksheet referenced the cell named COMMISSION, 1-2-3 would adjust all their results to reflect this one change. Powerful stuff!

Formulas That Make Decisions

There will be times when you want 1-2-3 to carry out one task under certain circumstances and another task if those circumstances don't apply. To give this kind of instruction to 1-2-3, you use the @IF function.

Using the @IF Function

How @IF works

In its simplest form, the @IF function tests the value of a cell and does one thing if the test is positive (true) and another if the test is negative (false). It requires three arguments: the test, the action to perform if the test is true, and the action to perform if the test is false. You supply the arguments one after the other within the function's parentheses, separating them with commas (no spaces). Try this:

1. Select cell D4, type the following, and then press Enter:

   @IF(B4=0,"TRUE","FALSE")

   1-2-3 checks whether the value in cell B4 is zero (the test), and because it isn't zero, it ignores TRUE (the action to perform if the test is true) and displays FALSE (the action to perform if the test is false) in cell D4.

2. With cell D4 selected, drag through =0 in the contents box to highlight it, type <*1000000*, and press Enter. The entry in cell D4 instantly changes from FALSE to TRUE, because the value in cell B4 is less than 1 million; that is, the test is true.

In this example, the test 1-2-3 performed was a simple evaluation of the value in a cell. However, you can also build tests that involve other functions. Recall that the last two characters of the invoice numbers in column B of the worksheet indicate whether the sale originated in your company's East or West office. Suppose you want to assign East and West entries to each invoice so that you can compare the performance of the two offices. Follow these steps:

1. Select cell D14, type *Office*, and press Down Arrow.

2. In cell D15, type the following and then press Down Arrow:

   @IF(@RIGHT(B15,2)="AA","East","West")

A function for every task

1-2-3 has over 200 @functions, 120 of which are new to Release 4. Many functions are provided for common business and financial tasks—some of them quite complex. To get more information about a function, choose Contents and then @Functions from the Help menu and follow the instructions given in the Help window.

You have told 1-2-3 to look at the two characters at the right end of the value in cell B15 and, if they are AA, to enter East in cell D15. If they are not AA, 1-2-3 is to enter West. Here's the result:

Using Nested @IF Functions

When constructing conditions, you can use @IF functions within @IF functions. Called *nested functions*, these formulas add another dimension to the complexity of the decisions 1-2-3 can make. Here's a quick demonstration:

> Functions within functions

1. Display the Editing SmartIcon palette by clicking the SmartIcon selector on the status bar and then clicking Editing.

> The Editing SmartIcon palette

2. Click the column B header and then click the Insert Columns icon to insert a new column.

3. In cell B3, type * and press Enter. Repeat this step for cell B11. Then enter the column heading *Quarter* in cell B14.

4. Select B15..B25, click the number format selector on the status bar, and select Automatic from the menu of number formats.

5. Now select cell B15 and type this formula all on one line:

@IF(@MONTH(A15)<4,1,@IF(@MONTH(A15)<7,2,
    @IF(@MONTH(A15)<10,3,4)))

6. Check your typing, paying special attention to all the parentheses, and then click the Confirm button.

You have told 1-2-3 to check the month component of the date in cell A15. If it is less than 4, 1-2-3 is to display 1 in the corresponding cell in the Quarter column. If the month is not less than 4 but is less than 7, 1-2-3 is to display 2 in the Quarter column. If it is not less than 7 but is less than 10, 1-2-3 is to display 3. Otherwise, 1-2-3 is to display 4. If you have typed the formula correctly, 1-2-3 enters 1 in cell B15.

Copying Formulas

The @IF functions you just entered are arduous to type, even for good typists. Fortunately, you don't have to enter them more than once. Using the Copy Down icon, you can copy the formula into the cells below, like this:

Copying down a range

1. Select B15..B25 and click the Copy Down icon. 1-2-3 copies the @IF formula into the selected range in column B.

2. Select E15..E25, click the Copy Down icon to copy the formula in cell E15, and scroll the worksheet to see the results:

	Date	Quarter	Invoice Number	Salesperson	Office	Amount of Sale
12	Invoice Details					
14	Date	Quarter	Invoice Number	Salesperson	Office	Amount of Sale
15	03/09/93	1	4739AA	Crux, Jamie	East	$83,456.2
16	01/04/93	1	943200	Olderon, Sam	West	$90,875.5
17	01/10/93	1	8488AA	Karnov, Peter	East	$63,456.8
18	01/16/93	1	4398AA	Sweldon, Chaz	East	$42,356.0
19	02/03/93	1	4945AA	Crux, Tad	East	$65,643.9
20	02/08/93	1	825600	Furban, Wally	West	$123,456.4
21	02/14/93	1	846500	Ladder, Larry	West	$67,345.2
22	03/02/93	1	4409AA	Karnov, Peter	East	$145,768.3
23	03/12/93	1	8867AA	Crux, Jamie	East	$43,256.2
24	03/23/93	1	875600	Ladder, Larry	West	$11,256.9
25	03/30/93	1	479300	Furban, Wally	West	$85,345.0

3. Click cell E15 and look at the formula in the contents box. 1-2-3 has changed the original formula

=@IF(@RIGHT(B15,2)="AA","East","West")

to

=@IF(@RIGHT(C15,2)="AA","East","West")

1-2-3 changed the reference to account for the addition of the Quarter column. If you click cell E16, you'll see that when you used the Copy Down icon, 1-2-3 changed the reference so that it refers to cell C16 for its argument, not C15.

By default, 1-2-3 uses *relative references* in its formulas. Relative references refer to cells by their position in relation to the cell containing the formula. So when you copied the formula in cell E15 to cell E16, 1-2-3 changed the reference from C15 to C16—the cell in the same row and two columns to the left of the cell containing the formula. If you were to copy the formula in cell E15 to F15, 1-2-3 would change the reference from C15 to D15 so that the formula would continue to reference the cell in the same relative position.

Relative references

When you don't want a reference to be copied as a relative reference, as it was in these examples, you need to use an *absolute reference*. Absolute references refer to cells by their fixed position in the worksheet. To make a reference absolute, you add dollar signs before its column letter and row number. For example, to change the reference C4..C9 to an absolute reference, you would enter it as C4..C9. You could then copy a formula that contained this reference anywhere on the worksheet and it would always refer to the range C4..C9.

Absolute references

References can also be partially relative and partially absolute. For example, $C3 has an absolute column reference and a relative row reference, and C$3 has a relative column reference and an absolute row reference.

Checking Spelling

In a moment, we'll print the INVOICES worksheet, but because you will usually want to spell-check your worksheets before you print them, we'll pause here to discuss 1-2-3's Spell Checker. You can check all or part of your worksheet for misspelled words and duplicate words within a block. From the Spell Check dialog box, you can edit the dictionary 1-2-3 uses to check your work, and you can add words to or delete words from it. In this section, we'll introduce a deliberate misspelling into the INVOICES worksheet and spell-check the worksheet to see how Spell Checker works.

1. Double-click cell A9 to edit its entry directly within the cell. Delete the *e* from the end of *Expense* and press Enter. Then press Home to move to A1.

2. Click the SmartIcon selector on the status bar and then click Printing. We will use this palette to access the Spell Checker and to perform printing tasks in the next section.

3. Click the Spell Check icon.

4. 1-2-3 starts checking the INVOICES worksheet, finds the misspelled word, and displays this dialog box:

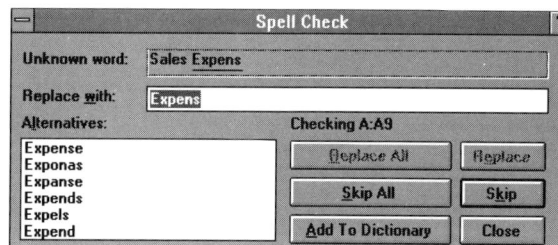

5. In the Alternatives list box, 1-2-3 suggests possible replacements for the misspelled word. Click Expense and then click the Replace button. The Spell Checker replaces the word and continues checking the document.

6. Complete the spell-check, clicking the Skip buttons for all other "misspellings." When the Spell Checker finishes checking the worksheet, it displays a message box.

7. Click OK to return to the worksheet.

Printing Worksheets

If your primary purpose in learning 1-2-3 is to be able to manipulate your own information and come up with results that will guide your decision-making, your worksheets might never need to leave your computer. If, on the other hand, you want to sway the decisions of your colleagues or you need to prepare reports for your board of directors, you will probably need printed copies of your worksheets. Now is a good time to discuss how to print a 1-2-3 document.

Checking one sheet or a selection

If you don't want to spell-check an entire worksheet, choose Spell Check from the Tools menu instead of clicking the Spell Check icon. 1-2-3 then displays a dialog box in which you can specify that you want to spell-check only the current sheet or only a selected range.

Previewing Worksheets

Usually, you will want to preview your worksheets before you print them to make sure that single-page documents fit neatly on the page and that multi-page documents break in logical places. You can choose the Preview command from the File menu or click the Preview icon to get a bird's-eye view of your document. Follow these steps to preview the INVOICES worksheet:

Bird's-eye view

1. Click the Preview icon. 1-2-3 displays this dialog box:

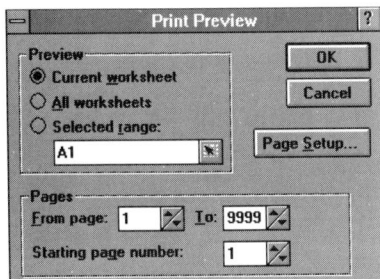

2. Click OK to preview the worksheet, which looks like this:

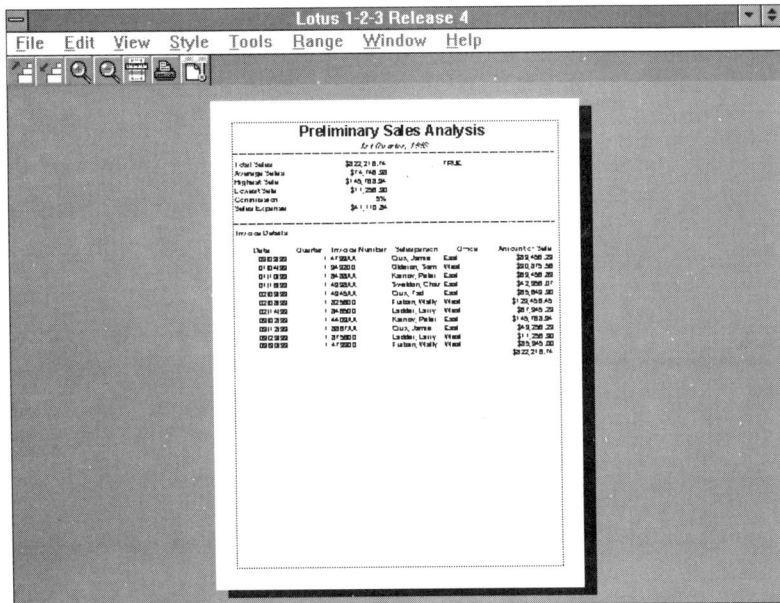

Printer setup

If your computer can access more than one printer, or if you need to set up a printer to print with 1-2-3, choose the Printer Setup command from the File menu. In the Printer Setup dialog box, click the Setup button and then make any necessary changes to the settings in the resulting dialog box before trying to print.

3. Click the first four icons on the Preview SmartIcon palette to see their effects. (We'll use the other three icons in a minute.)

4. When you are ready, click the Exit Preview icon or press the Esc key to return to the worksheet window.

Setting Up the Pages

For presentation purposes, you may want to make changes in the way 1-2-3 prints your worksheet. For example, you might want a header at the top and a footer at the bottom of each page or you might want to include the worksheet's column letters and row numbers or grid lines in the printout. You might want to print the worksheet horizontally (in landscape mode) instead of vertically (in portrait mode). You make these changes in the Page Setup dialog box, which you access either by choosing the Page Setup command from the File menu or by clicking the Page Setup icon. Follow these steps:

1. Click the Page Setup icon on the Printing SmartIcon palette to display this dialog box:

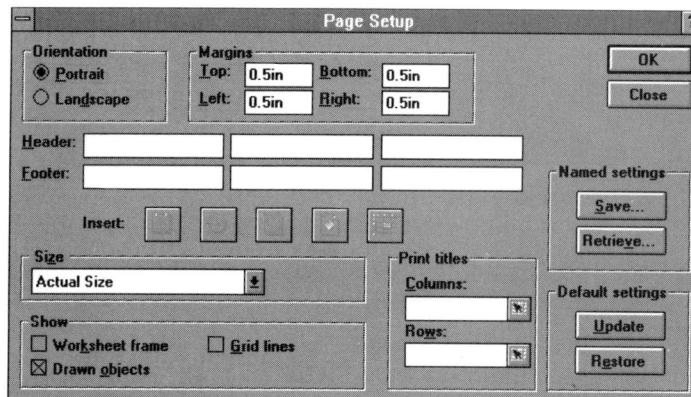

Printing on one page

Often, you can force 1-2-3 to print a worksheet on one page by manipulating the widths of columns. You can also use the Fit All To Page, Fit Columns To Page, Fit Rows To Page, or Manually Scale options in the Size section of the Page Setup dialog box. (The first three options have equivalent icons on the Printing SmartIcon palette.)

2. To print your worksheet horizontally across the width of the page, click the Landscape option in the Orientation section.

3. In the left Footer edit box, type *Last Revised*, a colon (:) and a space, and then click the first Insert icon (Insert Date).

4. In the center Footer edit box, type *SALES ANALYSIS*.

5. In the right Footer edit box, type *Page* and a space, and then click the third Insert icon (Insert Page Number). Click OK.

6. Click the Preview icon and then click OK to see the effects of these changes on your printout:

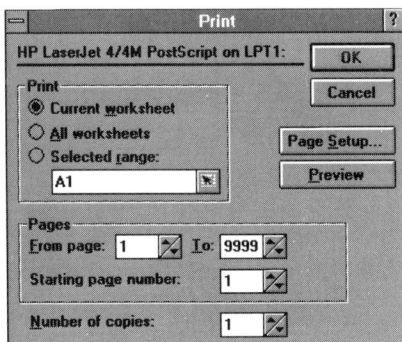

7. When you're ready, click the Exit Preview icon to return to the worksheet.

Preparing to Print

When you are ready to print, you choose Print from the File menu or click the Print icon to display this Print dialog box:

In this dialog box, you can adjust the print range and specify which pages you want to print in a multi-page document. You can also go directly to the Page Setup dialog box by clicking the Page Setup button, or to Print Preview by clicking the Preview button.

To send the worksheet to the printer, you simply click OK. You can then evaluate the results on paper.

Setting/removing page breaks

To print the calculation area on one page and the supporting data on another, or to control page breaks in a multi-page worksheet, select the cell below the row and to the right of the column at which you want to break the page, and either choose Page Break from the Style menu and select Row, Column, or both, or click the Horizontal Page Break or Vertical Page Break icons on the Printing SmartIcon palette. To remove a manual page break, select the cell immediately below and to the right of the break, choose the Page Break command from the Style menu, click any selected option to deselect it, and click OK.

Extracting Information
from a Database

What you will learn

Lotus 1-2-3 Release 4 - [INV_LOG.WK4]

File Edit View Style Tools Range Window Help

A:A1   ^Invoice Log

New Sheet

	A	B	C	D	E	F	G	H
1	Date	Quarter	Invoice	Salesperson	Office	Amount		
2	01/10/93	1	8488AA	Karnov, Peter	East	$63,456.83		
3	03/02/93	1	4409AA	Karnov, Peter	East	$145,768.34		
4	04/17/93	2	8488AA	Karnov, Peter	East	$63,456.83		
5	05/07/93	2	4409AA	Karnov, Peter	East	$145,768.34		
6	07/17/93	3	8488AA	Karnov, Peter	East	$63,456.83		
7	08/06/93	3	4409AA	Karnov, Peter	East	$145,768.34		
8	10/17/93	4	8488AA	Karnov, Peter	East	$63,456.83		
9	11/06/93	4	4409AA	Karnov, Peter	East	$145,768.34		

New Sheet

	A	B	C	D	E	F	G
1			**Invoice Log**				
2			*1993*				
3							
4	Date	Quarter	Invoice	Salesperson	Office	Amount	
5	03/09/93	1	4739AA	Crux, Jamie	East	$83,456.23	
6	01/04/93	1	943200	Olderon, Sam	West	$90,875.56	
7	01/10/93	1	8488AA	Karnov, Peter	East	$63,456.83	

Automatic   Arial MT   24 07/31/93 11:55 AM   Ready

We covered a lot of important ground in Chapter 2, and you now have a feel for some of the power of 1-2-3. In this chapter, we show you more techniques for efficient worksheet creation and management. Using an invoice log as a base worksheet, we describe how to sort and extract data and how to calculate statistics from a database. Let's start by creating the invoice log.

Cloning Worksheets

Using one worksheet as the basis for another is a very important time-saving technique. In this section, we will clone the INVOICES worksheet to create another worksheet called INV_LOG. Then we'll use a few tricks to transform the new worksheet into a simulated invoice log (a record of sales). If you need to create such a log for your work, you can key in real data. In Chapter 6, we show you how to automate the process of inputing this kind of information so that you are spared hours of typing. In the meantime, though, let's create a simulated log to give us a large worksheet to manipulate in the other sections of this chapter. Follow these steps to create INV_LOG:

1. Click the Open icon or choose Open from the File menu to display the File Open dialog box. The worksheet files stored in the 123R4W\SAMPLE directory are listed in the File Name list box. Click INVOICES.WK4 and then click OK to open the INVOICES worksheet.

Saving under a different filename

2. Choose Save As from the File menu to display the Save As dialog box.

3. In the File Name edit box, type *inv_log* and click OK. You now have two identical worksheets saved under different names.

A few alterations to INV_LOG will give you a usable sample worksheet:

1. In cell A1, type *Invoice Log* and press Down Arrow to enter the text in A1 and move the cell pointer down one cell. In A2, type *'1993*, and press Enter.

2. Select the headers for rows A3 through A12, right-click them to display the row quick menu, and choose Delete to remove the selected rows.

3. Select A5..F15, click the Copy icon, click cell A16, and click the Paste icon to insert the selected range of data.

4. Select A5..F26 and click the Copy icon again. Then press the PgDn key to scroll cell A27 into view, and click A27. Click the Paste icon to insert the selected range of data.

Let's revise some of the invoice dates so that the log includes invoices for all the months of the year. Rather than changing dates manually, we'll take this opportunity to demonstrate the Fill command on the Range menu. Later in this chapter, we'll use this command to create a sequential set of numbers. Here, we'll use it to create a set of evenly spaced dates. (This is, of course, just a simulation of a database. If you were logging real invoices in this database, you would use the actual sale dates.) Follow these steps:

1. Select A16..A26 and choose Fill from the Range menu. 1-2-3 displays this dialog box:

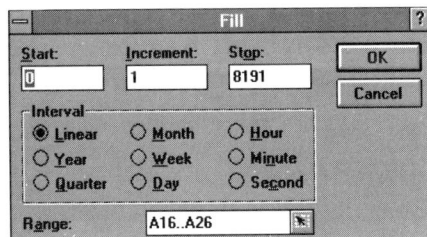

Creating a series of dates

2. Enter the date *04/09/93* in the Start edit box. Then enter *4* in the Increment edit box to tell 1-2-3 to create a range of dates in increments of four days. Enter the date *12/31/93* in the Stop edit box. Click OK to create the range of dates.

3. Select A27..A37 and again choose Fill from the Range menu. Notice that 1-2-3 has converted the dates you entered in the Start and Stop boxes into date values.

4. Type the new date *07/09/93* in the Start edit box and then click OK to create a new range of dates.

Date increments

You can use the Fill command on the Range menu to create a series of dates of almost any type. In the Interval section of the Fill dialog box, click one of the buttons to increment the range of dates by days, weeks, months, quarters, or years. You can also click for time increments of hours, minutes and seconds.

5. Select A38..A48 and choose Fill a third time.

6. Type *10/09/93* in the Start edit box and click OK.

7. Press the Home key. Notice that your worksheet now contains invoices for all four quarters of the year. The formulas in column B have done their work and assigned the invoices to quarters based on the dates in column A:

Selecting ranges across sheets

Occasionally you might want to perform an operation on a range of cells that extends across two or more consecutive sheets—a three-dimensional range. The reference for a three-dimensional range includes the names of the beginning and ending sheets. For example, A:A1..C:D5 refers to the ranges A1..D5 on sheets A, B, and C. If you want to select a three-dimensional range, use the F4 key. For example, to select A:A1..C:D5, begin by selecting A:A1..A:D5. Next, press F4 to anchor the range, press Ctrl-PgUp twice, and then press Enter. If you are in perspective view, you will see the selection in sheets A, B, and C.

This large worksheet is ideal for demonstrating some of 1-2-3's database features.

Sorting Data

The sales data in the worksheet you created in Chapter 2 fits neatly on one screen. To find out which salesperson from the West office has made the highest single sale, you could simply look at the worksheet. Getting that information from the worksheet now on your screen is a little more difficult. Fortunately, 1-2-3 can quickly sort worksheets like this one, using one, two, or more levels of sorting.

Adding Sort Codes

Before you sort any large worksheet, you should ask yourself whether you might need to put the data back in its original order. If there is even a chance that you will, you should add sort codes to the worksheet before you begin sorting. A *sort code* is a sequential number assigned to each row of entries. After changing the order of the entries, you can sort again on the basis of the sort code to put everything back where it was. Follow these steps to add sort codes to INV_LOG:

1. Right-click the header of column A to display the column quick menu and choose Insert to insert a blank column in front of the Date column.

2. Select cell A4, type *Sort Code*, and press Enter.

3. Select A5..A48 and choose Fill from the Range menu. In the Fill dialog box, notice that the Start, Increment, and Stop edit boxes still contain entries from the last time you used this command.

> Creating a series of numbers

4. Type *1* in the Start edit box and *1* in the Increment edit box. Then type *44* in the Stop edit box and click OK. 1-2-3 fills the selected range with sequential integers from 1 through 44, like this:

	A	B	C	D	E	F
5	1	03/09/93	1	4739AA	Crux, Jamie	East
6	2	01/04/93	1	943200	Olderon, Sam	West
7	3	01/10/93	1	8488AA	Karnov, Peter	East
8	4	01/16/93	1	4398AA	Sweldon, Chaz	East
9	5	02/03/93	1	4945AA	Crux, Tad	East
10	6	02/08/93	1	825600	Furban, Wally	West
11	7	02/14/93	1	846500	Ladder, Larry	West
12	8	03/02/93	1	4409AA	Karnov, Peter	East
13	9	03/12/93	1	8867AA	Crux, Jamie	East
14	10	03/23/93	1	875600	Ladder, Larry	West
15	11	03/30/93	1	479300	Furban, Wally	West
16	12	04/09/93	2	4739AA	Crux, Jamie	East
17	13	04/13/93	2	943200	Olderon, Sam	West
18	14	04/17/93	2	8488AA	Karnov, Peter	East
19	15	04/21/93	2	4398AA	Sweldon, Chaz	East
20	16	04/25/93	2	4945AA	Crux, Tad	East
21	17	04/29/93	2	825600	Furban, Wally	West
22	18	05/03/93	2	846500	Ladder, Larry	West
23	19	05/07/93	2	4409AA	Karnov, Peter	East
24	20	05/11/93	2	8867AA	Crux, Jamie	East

Lotus 1-2-3 Release 4 - [INV_LOG.WK4] — File Edit View Style Tools Range Window Help — A5..A48 — Automatic | Arial MT | 12 07/31/93 10:45 AM | Ready

Now let's look at various ways you might want to sort the INV_LOG worksheet.

Quick range selection

1-2-3 offers a quick keyboard technique for selecting a large range of contiguous data. Position the cell pointer in the top left corner of the range and press the End key. The word End appears in the status bar. Hold down the Shift key and press Right Arrow. Without releasing the Shift key, press End again and then Down Arrow. Release the Shift key. Pressing the End key instructs 1-2-3 to jump in the direction of the following Arrow key to the end of the range that contains data. Pressing the Shift key at the same time tells 1-2-3 to select the range over which you are moving the cell pointer.

Using One Sort Key

The simplest sorting procedure is based on only one column, or *sort key*. You indicate which column 1-2-3 should use, and the program rearranges the rows of the selected range accordingly. Let's start by sorting the data in INV_LOG by regional office so that you can see how the process works:

1. Select A5..G48 and choose Sort from the Range menu. 1-2-3 displays the Sort dialog box, which contains the reference A5..G48 in the Range edit box:

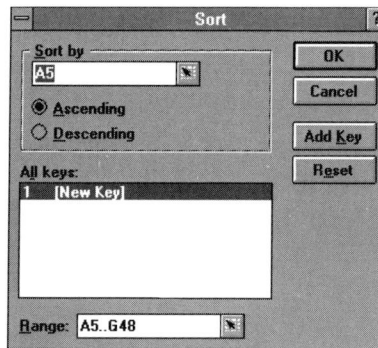

```
┌─────────────────────────────────────────────┐
│ ─                     Sort                  ? │
│  ┌─Sort by ──────────────────┐  ┌─────────┐  │
│  │ A5                      ▼ │  │   OK    │  │
│  │                           │  └─────────┘  │
│  │ ◉ Ascending               │  ┌─────────┐  │
│  │ ○ Descending              │  │ Cancel  │  │
│  └───────────────────────────┘  └─────────┘  │
│   All keys:                      ┌─────────┐  │
│  ┌───────────────────────────┐  │ Add Key │  │
│  │ 1  [New Key]              │  └─────────┘  │
│  │                           │  ┌─────────┐  │
│  │                           │  │  Reset  │  │
│  │                           │  └─────────┘  │
│  │                           │               │
│  └───────────────────────────┘               │
│   Range:  A5..G48         ▼                   │
└─────────────────────────────────────────────┘
```

2. In the Sort By edit box, you need to designate the column you want 1-2-3 to use as the basis for the upcoming one-key sort, so click the *range selector*—the pointer button—at the right end of this edit box. 1-2-3 moves you to the worksheet.

The range selector

3. Use the range selector pointer to click any cell in column F. A reference to that cell appears in the Sort By edit box.

4. By default, 1-2-3 selects Ascending as the sort order for the records. Click OK to sort the records with the current settings.

   The invoice data is now sorted alphabetically by regional office, with all the invoices for the East office coming before those for the West office.

Don't include headings

If you include row 4—the heading row—in the range to be sorted, 1-2-3 sorts the column headings along with the entries. As a result, the headings might end up in the middle of the worksheet instead of at the top of their respective columns.

Using Two Sort Keys

Now let's take things a step further and sort the invoices not only by regional office but also by salesperson:

1. With the range still highlighted, choose Sort from the Range menu. In the All Keys box is the key for the previous sort.

2. Click the range selector at the right end of the Sort By edit box, select a cell in column E to put its reference in the Sort By edit box, and click OK to close the Sort dialog box and sort the database table.

The invoice data is now sorted alphabetically by regional office and alphabetically within region by the names of the salespeople.

Using Three Sort Keys

Depending on the focus of your current analysis, you might want to sort INV_LOG based on the Date or Quarter columns. However, let's assume you are interested in each person's sales volume and add one more key to the sort. To sort by regional office, salesperson, and amount of invoice, follow these steps:

1. Choose Sort from the Range menu. Again, the Sort dialog box retains the selections from the previous sort.

2. Click the range selector at the right end of the Sort By edit box, click a cell in column G, and click OK.

Adjust the widths of columns A, B, and F so that columns A through G are visible. Now you can scroll the database to see the highest sale of each salesperson in each region:

Ascending and descending

The result of selecting Ascending or Descending in the Sort dialog box depends on the type of value used in the sort key. For alphabetic labels, Ascending is from *A* to *Z* and Descending is from *Z* to *A*. For dates or times, Ascending is from earliest to latest and Descending is from latest to earliest.

Freezing Headings

As you scroll through the invoice log to check how 1-2-3 has sorted the data, you'll probably find yourself wishing that the column headings hadn't scrolled out of sight. You can freeze the headings at the top of the screen like this:

Scrolling part of a worksheet →

1. Move the cell pointer to A5, and then choose Freeze Titles from the View menu to display the Freeze Titles dialog box:

```
┌─────────────────────────────┐
│ ─    Freeze Titles      ?   │
├─────────────────────────────┤
│  ● Rows          ┌────────┐ │
│  ○ Columns       │   OK   │ │
│                  └────────┘ │
│  ○ Both          ┌────────┐ │
│                  │ Cancel │ │
│                  └────────┘ │
└─────────────────────────────┘
```

2. Click OK to accept Row, the default selection.

3. Back on the worksheet, press the PgDn key to scroll through the data. The headings in row 4 remain in view while the rows below scroll up. In effect, the Freeze Titles command gives you views of two different portions of your worksheet, as you can see here:

#	A	B	C	D	E	F	G
1				**Invoice Log**			
2				*1993*			
3							
4	Sort Code	Date	Quarter	Invoice Number	Salesperson	Office	Amount of Sale
33	17	04/29/93	2	825600	Furban, Wally	West	$123,456.45
34	28	07/29/93	3	825600	Furban, Wally	West	$123,456.45
35	39	10/29/93	4	825600	Furban, Wally	West	$123,456.45
36	6	02/08/93	1	825600	Furban, Wally	West	$123,456.45
37	10	03/23/93	1	875600	Ladder, Larry	West	$11,256.90
38	32	08/14/93	3	875600	Ladder, Larry	West	$11,256.90
39	21	05/15/93	2	875600	Ladder, Larry	West	$11,256.90
40	43	11/14/93	4	875600	Ladder, Larry	West	$11,256.90

4. To turn off this scrolling feature, choose Clear Titles from the View menu.

Database Basics

The invoice log is an organized collection of information about invoices. By common definition, it is a *database*. A database is a table of related data with a rigid structure that

A splitting alternative

Another way to see two parts of a worksheet at once is to select a split location on your worksheet, choose Split from the View menu, select Horizontal, Vertical, or Perspective from the Split dialog box, and click OK. To restore your worksheet window to a single pane, select the Clear option in the Split dialog box.

enables you to easily locate and evaluate individual items of information. Each row of a database is a *record* that contains all the pertinent information about one component of the database. For example, row 5 of the invoice log contains all the information about one particular invoice. Each cell of the database is a *field* that contains one item of information. Cell G5, for instance, contains the amount of the invoice for the record in row 5. All the fields in a particular column contain the same kind of information about their respective records. For example, column B of the invoice log contains the dates of all the invoices. At the top of each column is a heading, called the *field name*.

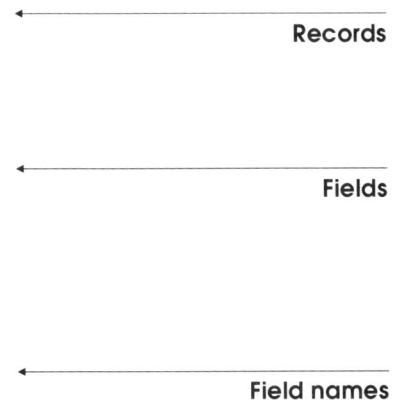

In the next sections, we'll cover 1-2-3's database capabilities. First, however, follow these steps to restore the invoice log to its original order and to make a few other necessary adjustments:

1. Select A5..G48, choose Sort from the Range menu, and click the Reset button to erase the current key definitions. Click the range selector at the right end of the Sort By edit box, click a cell in column A, and click OK. 1-2-3 sorts the database records back into their original positions.

2. Right-click the column A header to display the column quick menu and choose Delete. The invoice log now contains only its original six columns.

3. Because each field name in a 1-2-3 database must consist of only a single word with no spaces, you now need to revise two of the headings at the top of the columns containing invoice data. Select cell C4 and reenter the heading as *Invoice*. Then select cell F4 and enter *Amount* as the new heading.

4. You also need to delete the range name AMOUNT assigned earlier to the sales amounts. (The name is not relevant to the database and will conflict with the Amount field name in some database operations.) To delete the name, choose Name from the Range menu, highlight AMOUNT in the Existing Named Ranges list box, click the Delete button, and then click OK to close the dialog box.

Records

Fields

Field names

Field-name conventions

1-2-3 imposes several rules on the format of field names for a database. Each name must consist of a one-word label with no spaces. Avoid special characters that might make a field name resemble an address reference. No two field names can be the same; in addition, a field name should not be the same as a name defined for a range in the same worksheet.

Assigning a name to the database

To simplify your work with the invoice records, let's assign a range name to the entire database, including the row of field names:

1. Select A4..F48, choose Name from the Range menu, type the name *invdb* (for "invoice database") in the Name edit box, and click OK.

2. Press the Home key to return to cell A1, and then click the Save icon to save the current version of the invoice log.

You are now ready to begin exploring 1-2-3's database operations, which you perform by choosing the Database command from the Tools menu. As you'll see in the following sections, the options in the Database menu give you ways to query, find, delete, and modify database records that match the criteria you define.

Finding and Deleting Records

You can tell 1-2-3 to find and highlight the records in the database that meet the criteria you specify. Let's try this now:

Finding records

1. Choose Database from the Tools menu to display this cascade menu:

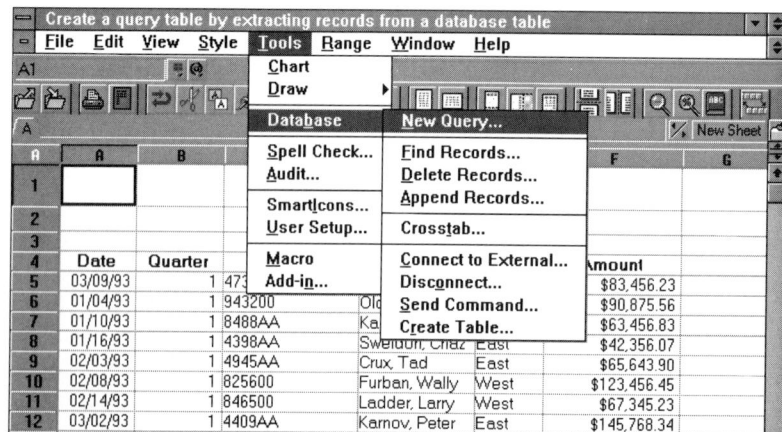

The commands on this menu allow you to manipulate your database records and connect to other databases.

2. Choose Find Records from the Database cascade menu to display the Find Records dialog box:

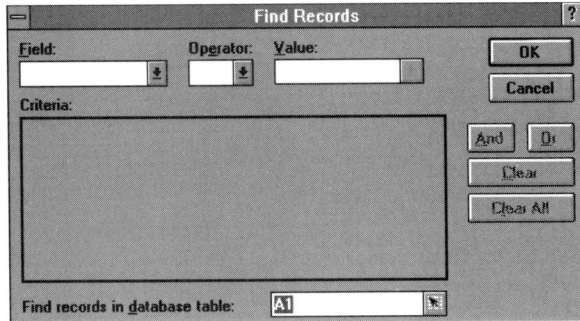

3. Click the range selector at the right end of the Find Records In Database Table edit box. On the worksheet, click the navigator to display the names defined for this worksheet, and select INVDB to identify the database you want to use. 1-2-3 enters the name in the edit box.

4. We want to find all the records for Jamie Crux, so start by clicking the down arrow at the right end of the Field edit box, and select Salesperson from the drop-down list box. 1-2-3 starts building the find criteria in the Criteria box below.

5. By default, 1-2-3 enters = in the Operator edit box and Crux, Jamie—the first name in the Salesperson column—in the Value edit box. Click OK to accept the criteria. 1-2-3 highlights the records that match the criteria, as shown here:

Viewing found records

6. Use the window's scroll bar to view the records and then press any key to remove the highlighting.

Deleting records

Choosing Database and then Delete Records from the Tools menu displays the Delect Records dialog box in which you can specify criteria for deleting records. When you click OK, 1-2-3 immediately removes all records that match the criteria from the database. If you change your mind right away, you can undo the deletion by clicking the Undo icon.

Manipulating Records

Suppose you invested a considerable chunk of your advertising budget for the year on a direct-mail flyer about a two-week promotion. For another two-week promotion earlier in the year, you relied on your salespeople to get the word out to their customers. You want to compare sales during the two promotions. Or suppose you want to analyze all sales over $60,000 to see if you can detect sales patterns. In either case, you can tell 1-2-3 to extract all the relevant invoices for scrutiny. You give 1-2-3 instructions of this kind by defining criteria in the Set Criteria dialog box. For example, you might tell 1-2-3 to find all the records with amounts over $60,000 by entering *>60000* as the criteria.

Adding a Sheet for the Query Table

Because 1-2-3 allows you to create multiple sheets within a single file, it's a good idea to locate the results of your database queries in a separate sheet so that they are easy to find and don't interfere with your database. Let's insert sheet B in the INV_LOG.WK4 file:

1. Click the New Sheet button at the right end of the tab line. 1-2-3 inserts the new sheet and displays it on your screen.

Using the sheet tabs, you can move easily between the sheets.

Creating a Query Table

To create a query table, you use the New Query dialog box to specify the database to be queried, the database fields and criteria to be used in the query, and the location of the query table where 1-2-3 outputs the results of the query. You can then work with the results by performing other queries. Follow these steps to create a table:

1. With cell B:A1 selected, choose Database and then New Query from the Tools menu to display this dialog box:

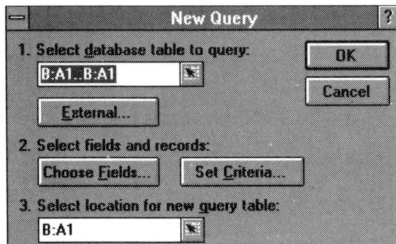

2. Click the range selector at the right end of the Select Database Table To Query edit box. Then click the navigator and select INVDB to identify the database you want to query.

Identifying the database

3. Click the Set Criteria button to display this dialog box:

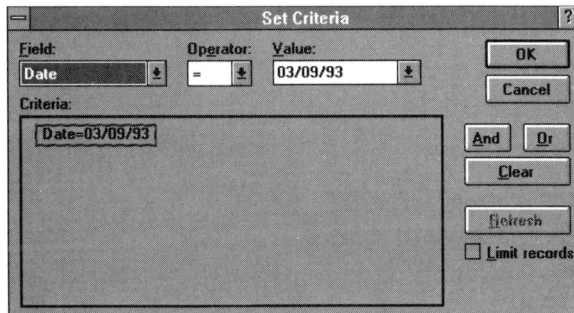

4. We want to see all the records that are for Peter Karnov *and* that have amounts over $60,000, so start by selecting the Salesperson field from the Field drop-down list box, leave the = entry in the Operator edit box as it is, and select Karnov, Peter from the Value drop-down list box. The criteria in the Criteria box now reads *Salesperson=Karnov, Peter*.

5. Click the And button. The box holding the criteria expands to include a second criteria.

6. Select Amount from the Field drop-down list box, select > (greater than) from the Operator drop-down list box, and type 60000 in the Value edit box. The Set Criteria dialog box now looks like the one on the next page.

Comparison operators

You can use these comparison operators to compute criteria:

= > < >= <= <>

You can also use the DOS * and ? wildcards in the Value edit box of the Set Criteria dialog box to match unspecified characters, and you can use @functions, and formulas.

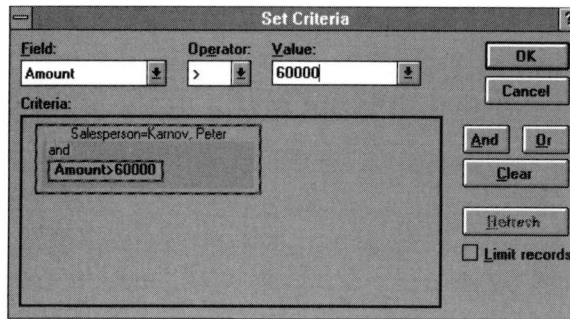

7. Click OK to return to the New Query dialog box. The location for the query table is already specified, so click OK again. 1-2-3 runs the query and displays these results in the query table in sheet B:

When the cell pointer is positioned in a query table, 1-2-3 replaces the Range menu with the Query menu on the menu bar and displays the Query SmartIcon palette. Some of its SmartIcons are familiar and some are new. You can get a feel for what they do by right-clicking each icon to display its description.

Some of the information in the query table is hidden because the columns are too narrow. Let's take a moment to adjust the column widths before we move on:

1. Select cell B:F1. 1-2-3 highlights the entire table column. Then click the Fit Widest Entry icon.

2. Select cell B:D1, click the Fit Widest Entry icon, and press Home. Now all the query results are visible:

Combining And and Or

To find first-quarter and second-quarter invoices for Peter Karnov, you enter three different criteria in the Set Criteria dialog box. Using the Field, Operator, and Value edit boxes, first specify *Salesperson = Karnov, Peter*. Then click the And button and specify *Quarter = 1*. Finally, click the Or button and specify *Quarter = 2*.

Updating Database Records

You can edit the records in a query table and then tell 1-2-3 to make the same changes to the records in your database. Before we see how this works, we'll split the window so that we can view both sheet A and sheet B at the same time and see the changes as they are made. Here are the steps:

1. Point to the splitting icon on the scroll bar, hold down the mouse button, and drag the icon to the bottom of row 11.

Splitting the window

2. In the bottom "pane," click tab A to display the worksheet in the bottom part of the window, and if necessary, press Home. Your screen now looks like this:

Preserving extracted records

When you extract records, 1-2-3 clears any previously extracted records in the same query table. If you want to preserve a set of extracted records, be sure to move the records elsewhere, or create a new query table for the next extraction.

To be able to update records in the database table, you need to set a query option before you make any modifications to the records in the query table. (You will need to reselect this option whenever you want to update records because 1-2-3 automatically deselects it after you update the database.) Follow these steps:

1. Click anywhere in the query table and choose Set Options from the Query menu to display the Set Options dialog box:

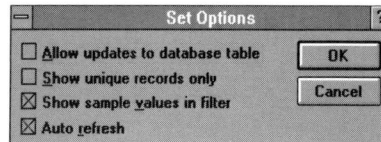

```
┌──────────── Set Options ──────────┐ ?
│ □ Allow updates to database table    ┌──────┐
│ □ Show unique records only           │  OK  │
│ ⊠ Show sample values in filter       └──────┘
│ ⊠ Auto refresh                       ┌──────┐
│                                      │Cancel│
│                                      └──────┘
└────────────────────────────────────┘
```

2. Select Allow Updates To Database Table and click OK. When 1-2-3 displays a warning that the option is turned on, click OK again.

Now let's edit the query table:

Editing the query table

1. Double-click C2 and change the invoice number to 8490AA. Then double-click F2 and change the amount to $65,394.55.

2. Click anywhere in the query table and choose Update Database Table from the Query menu. 1-2-3 updates the corresponding records in the database table to reflect your changes in the query table.

3. To get rid of the split window, drag the scroll bar's splitting icon to the top of your screen. The highlighted query table should now be on your screen.

4. Choose Refresh Now from the Query menu to ensure that all edits have been recorded.

Modifying Query Tables

Now that you have created a query table, you can reuse the table to perform other database operations without having to go through the whole query process again. Follow these steps to remove some fields from the query table and then specify other criteria:

Updating query table records

As you update records in your database, you can have 1-2-3 update them in a query table without having to rerun the query. Simply click the query table and choose the Refresh Now command from the Query menu. 1-2-3 updates the information in the query table to reflect the database.

1. Click the Choose Fields icon to display this dialog box:

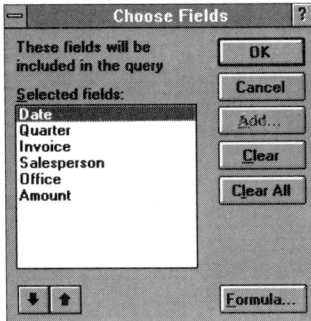

Choose Fields	?
These fields will be included in the query	OK
Selected fields:	Cancel
Date Quarter Invoice Salesperson Office Amount	Add... Clear Clear All
↓ ↑	Formula...

2. With Date highlighted in the Selected Fields list, click the Clear button. 1-2-3 deletes the Date field from the list.

Deleting fields from the query table

3. Select Invoice and click Clear, and then select Office and click Clear again. Now only three fields remain in the Selected Fields list box.

4. Select Salesperson and click the Up Arrow button below the Selected Fields list box to move that field to the top of the list.

5. Click OK to display the results in the query table. (Resize the columns as necessary using the Fit Widest Entry icon.)

Lotus 1-2-3 Release 4 - [INV_LOG.WK4]

File   Edit   View   Style   Tools   Query   Window   Help

Query 1

	A	B	C	D	E	F	G
1	Salesperson	Quarter	Amount				
2	Karnov, Peter	1	$65,394.55				
3	Karnov, Peter	1	$145,768.34				
4	Karnov, Peter	2	$63,456.83				
5	Karnov, Peter	2	$145,768.34				
6	Karnov, Peter	3	$63,456.83				
7	Karnov, Peter	3	$145,768.34				
8	Karnov, Peter	4	$63,456.83				
9	Karnov, Peter	4	$145,768.34				
10							
11							
12							
13							
14							

To select all the invoices for both Peter Karnov and Wally Furban, try this:

1. Click the Set Criteria icon to display the Set Criteria dialog box, which contains the criteria you used to create the current query table.

Removing criteria

2. Click the Clear button to remove the last criterion you specified and then click the Or button to add a new criterion.

3. Click the down arrow at the right end of the Value edit box and select Furban, Wally from the drop-down list. The Set Criteria dialog box now looks like this:

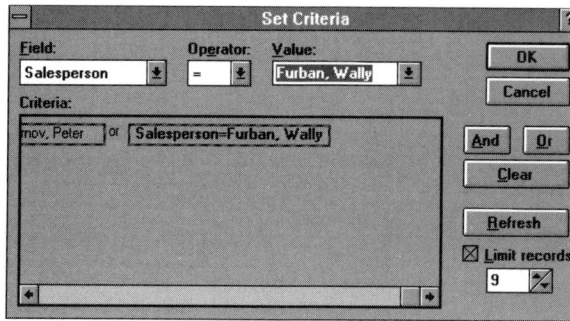

4. Click OK. As you can see, the query table now contains all the invoices for both salespeople:

Summarizing Aggregate Data

1-2-3 can calculate totals and other statistical values for the selected records in the query table. You select the column you want to calculate and choose the appropriate computation. As an example, we'll total the quarterly sales for the two salespeople whose records have been extracted into the query table. Follow these steps:

Other aggregate operations

In addition to Sum, the aggregate feature supports four other operations: Average, Maximum, Minimum, and Count. These operations work the same way as Sum. To perform one of these operations, first reset the data back to its original order by clicking the Reset button in the Aggregate dialog box. Then follow steps 1 through 4 on page 83, selecting an option other than Sum in step 3.

1. Select cell C1 to indicate which column you want to total.

2. Click the Aggregate icon to display this dialog box:

```
┌─────────── Aggregate ──────────┐
│ ┌─Compute──────────┐  ┌──OK──┐ │
│ │ ○ Sum   ○ Min    │           │
│ │ ○ Avg   ○ Max    │  ┌Cancel┐ │
│ │ ○ Count          │           │
│ └──────────────────┘  ┌Reset┐  │
│ Show field as:                 │
│ [Amount]                       │
│ For unique values of:          │
│ Quarter, Salesperson           │
└────────────────────────────────┘
```

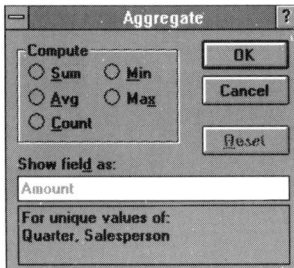

3. Click Sum. The Show Field As entry changes from Amount to Total Amount, the heading for the totals column.

4. Click OK. 1-2-3 totals the amounts by salesperson and quarter, and after widening the Total Amount column, you see these results:

	Salesperson	Quarter	Total Amount
1			
2	Furban, Wally	1	$208,801.45
3	Furban, Wally	2	$208,801.45
4	Furban, Wally	3	$208,801.45
5	Furban, Wally	4	$208,801.45
6	Karnov, Peter	1	$211,162.89
7	Karnov, Peter	2	$209,225.17
8	Karnov, Peter	3	$209,225.17
9	Karnov, Peter	4	$209,225.17

You can undo the aggregate operation and restore the records in the query table to their previous state, like this:

1. With the Total Amount column selected, click the Aggregate icon to display the Aggregate dialog box, which retains its previous settings.

2. Click the Reset button and then click OK. The original Amount column is restored in the query table.

As you have seen, 1-2-3's database commands are powerful tools to have at your disposal as you create and work with your own databases in 1-2-3.

Cross-tabulating data

In addition to aggregating data, you can also cross-tabulate it to produce a table of data summarized in the way you specify. For example, you can use the Crosstab command on the Database cascade menu to tell 1-2-3 to build a table with sales amounts totaled by salesperson and by quarter, with the salespeople in rows and the quarters in columns.

Visually Presenting Data

What you will learn

1993 BUDGET	1st Quarter	2nd Quarter	3rd Quarter	4th Quarter	Total
Sales	$522,216.74	$763,327.58	$804,438.41	$945,549.25	$3,035,531.98
Selling Expenses	$156,665.02	$228,998.27	$241,331.52	$283,664.78	$910,659.59
Marketing Expenses	$52,221.67	$76,332.76	$80,443.84	$94,554.93	$303,553.20
Overhead	$104,443.35	$152,665.52	$160,887.68	$189,109.85	$607,106.40
Total Expenses	$313,330.04	$457,996.55	$482,663.05	$567,329.55	$1,821,319.19
Net Income	$208,886.70	$305,331.03	$321,775.36	$378,219.70	$1,214,212.79

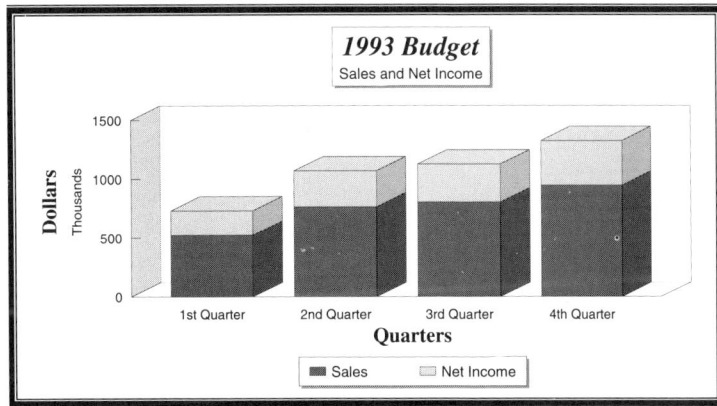

1993 Budget
Sales and Net Income

In the previous chapters, you learned a lot about 1-2-3 for Windows, and you now know enough to put 1-2-3 to use in your own work. After all that effort, let's relax a bit in this chapter. Using a budget worksheet as a basis, we'll explore the various ways you can visually present your worksheet data.

Setting Up a Budget

Before we can start, we need to set up this projected budget worksheet:

Once the worksheet is in place, we can plot the budget information as various kinds of charts. Assuming that you have started Windows and Lotus 1-2-3 for Windows, follow these steps to create the worksheet:

1. Close any open worksheets by choosing Close from the File menu or by clicking the worksheet's Control menu icon—the gray box with the small fat hyphen at the left end of the menu bar. 1-2-3 automatically supplies you with a new blank worksheet. If necessary, click the Maximize button to expand the worksheet window to fill the available space.

2. Save the blank worksheet as BUDGET.WK4. From now on, save the worksheet frequently as you build the budget.

**The Goodies
SmartIcon palette**

3. Click the SmartIcon selector on the status bar and select Goodies to display the Goodies SmartIcon palette.

4. In cell A1, type the title *1993 BUDGET* and press Right Arrow to enter the label and select cell B1.

5. In cell B1, type *1st Quarter*, and press Right Arrow. Then enter *2nd Quarter*, *3rd Quarter*, and *4th Quarter* in cells C1..E1. Finally, enter *Total* in cell F1.

6. Select A1..F1 and choose Column Width from the Style menu. When the Column Width dialog box appears, type *11* in the Set Width To edit box, and click OK. All six selected columns take on the new width.

7. In cell A2, type *Sales* and press Right Arrow.

8. Next, enter these sales amounts in the indicated cells:

B2	522216.74
C2	763327.58
D2	804438.41
E2	945549.25

Now let's tackle the expenses. To simplify the data entry process for this example, let's assume that we have selling expenses that average 30 percent of sales, marketing expenses that average 10 percent of sales, and overhead expenses (fixed costs) that average 20 percent.

1. Enter the following information in the indicated cells:

A4	Selling Expenses
A5	Marketing Expenses
A6	Overhead
A7	Total Expenses
A9	Net Income
B4	.3*B2
B5	.1*B2
B6	.2*B2
B7	@SUM(B4..B6)

For the entry in cell B7 you can either enter the @SUM function from the keyboard, or you can click the @function selector, select SUM from the list, and supply the range argument (see page 52 for more information).

2. Widen column A so that all its labels are visible.

3. Select the range B4..E7 and right-click the range to display its quick menu. Choose Copy Right. 1-2-3 copies the 1st quarter formulas into the columns for the 2nd, 3rd, and 4th quarters. Because the formulas in column B all contain relative references, 1-2-3 automatically adjusts the references as necessary to create new formulas for columns C, D, and E. (Examine the copied formulas to verify that they are correct.)

4. Select B2..F9, click the number format selector on the status bar, and select Currency.

Now, let's compute the Total column and Net Income row:

1. In cell B9, type *+B2–B7* and press Enter. 1-2-3 enters the result, $208,886.70, as the 1st quarter's net income.

2. Select B9..F9, right-click the range to display its quick menu, and choose Copy Right. 1-2-3 copies the formula in cell B9 to the cells in C9..F9. Once again, 1-2-3 makes appropriate adjustments in the relative references from the original formula to create the new formulas.

3. In cell F2, type *@SUM(B2..E2)* and press Enter.

4. Point to the bottom border of cell F2, hold down Ctrl, and drag the cell image to F4. When you release the mouse button, the @SUM function is copied to the specified location.

5. Select F4..F7, right-click the range, and choose Copy Down to copy the formula down the selected range.

Voilà! Your worksheet should look like the one shown earlier.

Fancy Formatting

Style templates

Now let's look at a powerful 1-2-3 feature designed to make short work of worksheet formatting: *style templates*. You have seen that you can use combinations of fonts and styles to draw attention to important worksheet details. A style template is a predefined combination of formatting that works well with worksheets like the one we just created to produce fancy-looking reports with the click of an icon. Try this:

1. Select A1..F9 and click the Style Template icon. 1-2-3 displays this dialog box:

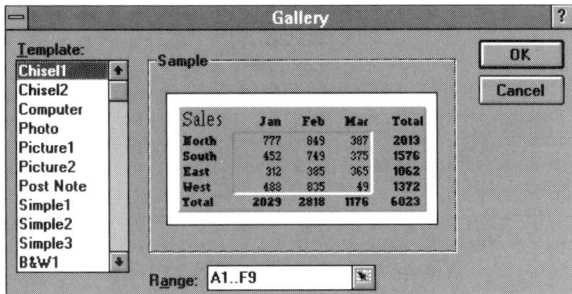

```
┌──────────────────────── Gallery ────────────────────[?]─┐
│ Template:                                                │
│ ┌────────┐  ┌─Sample──────────────────┐    ┌────────┐   │
│ │Chisel1▲│  │                          │    │   OK   │   │
│ │Chisel2 │  │                          │    └────────┘   │
│ │Computer│  │  Sales  Jan  Feb  Mar Total │  ┌────────┐   │
│ │Photo   │  │  North  777  849  387  2013 │  │ Cancel │   │
│ │Picture1│  │  South  452  749  375  1576 │  └────────┘   │
│ │Picture2│  │  East   312  385  365  1062 │               │
│ │Post Note│ │  West   488  835   49  1372 │               │
│ │Simple1 │  │  Total 2029 2818 1176  6023 │               │
│ │Simple2 │  └──────────────────────────┘               │
│ │Simple3 │                                               │
│ │B&W1   ▼│                                                │
│ └────────┘  Range: [A1..F9        ][▼]                   │
└──────────────────────────────────────────────────────────┘
```

2. Click OK to apply the Chisel1 template to the selected range. Here's the impressive result:

```
┌──────── Lotus 1-2-3 Release 4 - [BUDGET.WK4] ────────┐
│ File  Edit  View  Style  Tools  Range  Window  Help  │
│ A1..F9           ╪ ⓐ        '1993 BUDGET             │
│ [toolbar icons]                                       │
│ A                                      %  New Sheet   │
│     A              B          C          D          E          F        │
│ 1  1993 BUDGET   1st Quarter 2nd Quarter 3rd Quarter 4th Quarter    Total│
│ 2  Sales         $522,216.74 $763,327.58 $804,438.41 $945,549.25 $3,035,531.98│
│ 3                                                                         │
│ 4  Selling Expenses $156,665.02 $228,998.27 $241,331.52 $283,664.78 $910,659.59│
│ 5  Marketing Expenses $52,221.67 $76,332.76 $80,443.84 $94,554.93 $303,553.20│
│ 6  Overhead      $104,443.35 $152,665.52 $160,887.68 $189,109.85 $607,106.40│
│ 7  Total Expenses $313,330.04 $457,996.55 $482,663.05 $567,329.55 $1,821,319.19│
│ 8                                                                         │
│ 9  Net Income    $208,886.70 $305,331.03 $321,775.36 $378,219.70 $1,214,212.79│
│ 10                                                                        │
│ 11                                                                        │
│ 12                                                                        │
│ 13                                                                        │
└──────────────────────────────────────────────────────────────────────────┘
```

3. Click the Print icon to print the budget data.

4. Now click the Style Template icon again, select Picture1 from the Template list box, and click OK to produce another eye-catching report.

5. Try out some of the other templates, finishing with Simple2.

The style templates that come with 1-2-3 don't work well unless your worksheet is set up with them in mind. Nevertheless, they are a great way to become familiar with the many effects you can create with combinations of fonts, lines, colors, and shading. If you don't find a template that produces exactly the look you want, you can assign a template as a starting point and then make refinements using the Fonts & Attributes, Lines & Color, and Alignment commands.

Removing style templates

If you decide not to use a style template after all, the easiest way to remove all the formatting is to select the cells to which you have applied the template and choose Clear from the Edit menu. In the Clear dialog box, click Styles Only and then click OK. 1-2-3 resets the styles of the selected cells to the worksheet's default settings. Any manual formatting you have made is lost in addition to the template formatting.

Plotting Charts

With 1-2-3, you create charts on the worksheet. You can then save and print the chart and the underlying worksheet as one document. In this section, we show you how to quickly plot your data and work with a chart. We'll create the chart using the Chart icon, which automates the otherwise complex process of plotting data.

Dynamic links

When you create a chart from a selected range of data in a worksheet, 1-2-3 maintains a link between the worksheet and the chart. This link is dynamic: If you make changes to the worksheet data, 1-2-3 revises the chart to reflect the new data. You can create more than one chart from the same range of data, and the data can be arranged either in columns or rows. The first chart we'll create is a column-oriented chart.

1. Select A4..E6 and click the Chart icon.

2. Move the chart pointer to the blank area below your budget, hold down the mouse button, and drag to create a *marquee*—a dotted box—about the size of the worksheet window. (Don't worry about the precise size and location for now.) When you release the mouse button, 1-2-3 draws a bar chart of the expense data in the range you selected:

X-axis and y-axis

1-2-3 labels the x-axis and the y-axis on most charts. The x-axis shows the information categories—for example, sales and expenses. The y-axis shows the plotted data points (values).

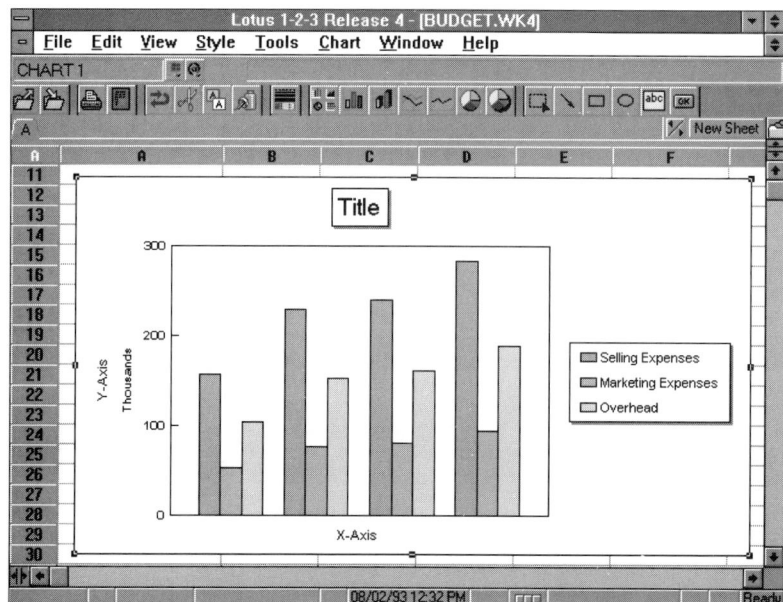

As you can see, four groups of vertical bars represent the four quarters of expense data. Within each group, three colors represent the three expense categories. To the right of the chart is a legend with the three labels from column A of the selected range: Selling Expenses, Marketing Expenses, and Overhead.

When a chart is selected, the Chart menu replaces the Range menu in the menu bar, and 1-2-3 displays the Chart SmartIcon palette to fascilitate your work with charts. You might want to take a couple of minutes to browse through the Chart menu and check out the icons on the palette before we move on.

The Chart SmartIcon palette

Sizing and Moving Charts

As we mentioned, you don't have to worry about the precise size and location of your chart when you create it because you can always adjust them by dragging the small black squares, called *handles*, around the chart's perimeter. Try this:

Handles

1. Point to the handle in the middle of the left side of the chart and drag it toward the center. 1-2-3 redraws the chart within a skinnier frame.

2. Drag a corner handle diagonally to change both the height and the width proportionally.

3. When you've finished experimenting, reshape the chart so that it occupies almost the entire window.

4. Now move the pointer into the blank area above the legend, hold down the mouse button, and drag the chart downward until the image of its top border sits at about row 32. When you release the mouse button, the chart snaps into its new location.

Naming Charts

If your chart is located some distance from its data, or if you have more than one chart on the same worksheet, it's useful to have a way to jump directly to the chart whenever you need to see a graphic representation of your data. With 1-2-3, you can assign a name to your chart, just as you can to cells and ranges (see page 41). Follow the steps on the next page.

1. With the chart selected, choose Name from the Chart menu to display the Name dialog box.

2. In the Chart Name edit box, type *expenses*, and click Rename. Back in the window, 1-2-3 displays the name EXPENSES in the selection indicator at the left end of the formula bar whenever the chart is selected.

   Now let's put this name to use:

Jumping to a named chart

1. Press the Home key to move to cell A1 of the worksheet and then choose Go To from the Edit menu to display the Go To dialog box:

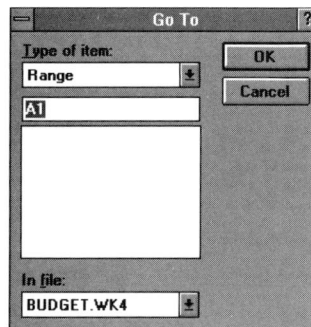

[Go To dialog box: Type of item: Range; A1; In file: BUDGET.WK4; OK; Cancel]

2. Click the down arrow at the right end of the Type Of Item edit box and select Chart from the drop-down list box. EX-PENSES is already highlighted—it's the only chart name you've defined—so click OK to jump directly to the chart.

Updating Charts

1-2-3 has actively linked your chart to its underlying data, so if you change the data, 1-2-3 automatically redraws the chart to reflect the change. Try this:

1. Press Home, select cell E2 on the worksheet, and reenter the 4th-quarter sales figure as *123456.78*. All the formulas go to work producing drastic changes in the expenses and net income amounts.

Chart scale

If you change the source data radically, the scale of the entire chart might change. For example, if you enter a sales amount in the millions in BUDGET.WK4, the other columns shrink down to almost nothing to keep the scale consistent.

2. Choose Go To from the Edit menu, select Chart from the Type Of Item drop-down list box, and click OK to jump to the chart named EXPENSES. As you can see, your change is immediately reflected in the chart:

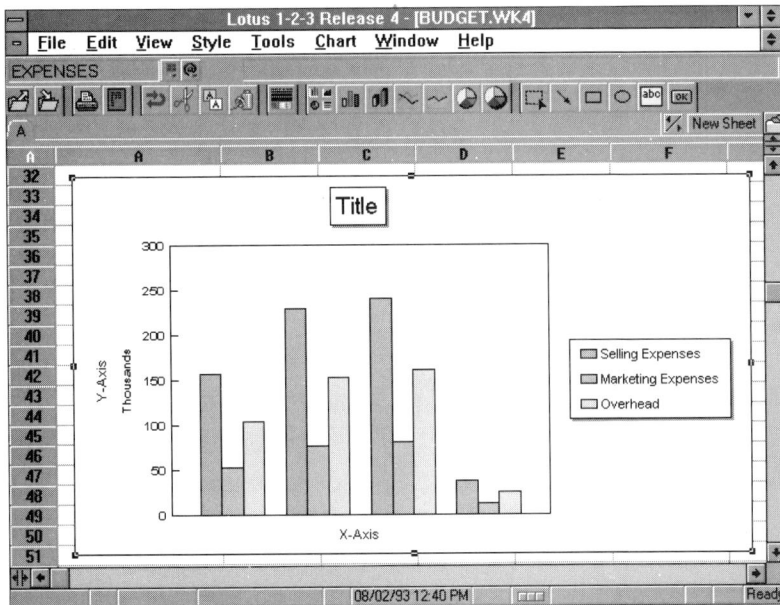

3. Click the Undo icon to restore the original 4th-quarter amounts.

Changing the Chart Type

Now that we've covered the basics of chart building, let's plot a new chart from the quarterly sales data so that we can explore the many charting possibilities available in 1-2-3. We'll start by deleting this chart and creating a new one:

1. With the expenses chart selected, press the Delete key. 1-2-3 removes the chart from the worksheet.

2. Press Home and then select B1..E2. The first row in this range contains labels that identify the four quarters of the budget year, and the second row contains numeric sales data.

3. Click the Chart icon and drag a window-sized marquee below the budget data. 1-2-3 draws the chart shown on the next page.

Underlying values

The format of the values in your worksheet does not affect the way they are plotted. 1-2-3 always uses the underlying values when plotting charts.

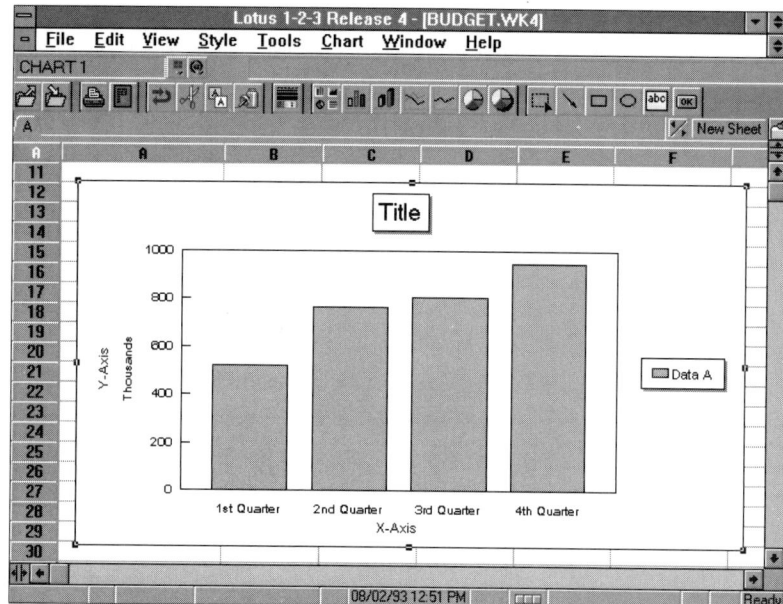

No matter what type of chart you need—bar, pie, line, and so on—1-2-3 has a format that will probably do the job. You can always come up with impressive visual support for a worksheet by carefully selecting from among 1-2-3's many predefined chart types. When a chart is active, you can change the chart type by clicking one of the dozen chart-type SmartIcons or by choosing Type from the Chart menu. The available types include:

Bar charts

- Bar charts, which are ideal for showing the variations in the value of an item over time, as with the budget example; or for showing the values of several items at a single point in time. In addition to the simple bar chart example that you've already seen, you can also create stacked or clustered bar charts, arranged either vertically or horizontally.

Line charts

- Line charts, which are often used to show variations in the value of more than one item over time.

Area charts

- Area charts, which look something like line charts but which plot multiple data series as cumulative layers with different colors, patterns, or shades.

Pie charts

- Pie charts, which are ideal for showing the percentages of an item that can be assigned to the item's components. (Pie charts can represent only one data range.)

- XY charts, which are used to detect correlations between independent items (such as a person's height and weight).

XY charts

- Mixed charts, which display some data ranges as bars and others as superimposed line charts.

Mixed charts

- HLCO ("high-low close-open") charts, which are typically used to plot stock-market activity.

HLCO charts

For bar charts, line charts, area charts, and pie charts, 1-2-3 also offers three-dimensional formats, augmenting the rich variety of visual representations you can choose for your data. Let's try changing the type of the current chart so that you can explore some of these possibilities:

1. With the chart selected, click the first Pie-Chart icon. 1-2-3 draws a chart in which the four quarters of sales data are represented as colored wedges in a circular pie. Next to each wedge, 1-2-3 displays the percentage of the whole represented by the wedge:

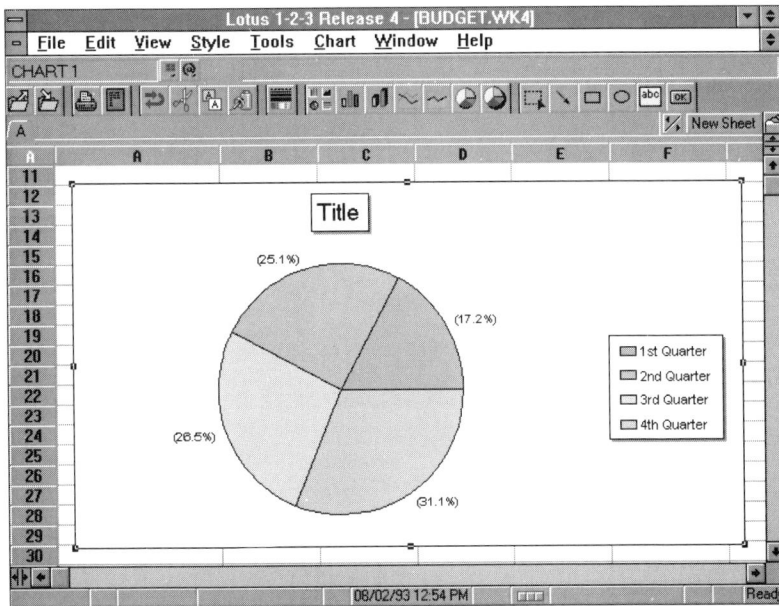

2. Click the Bar-Chart Icon to restore the previous chart format.

Let's add another set of data—the net income amounts—to the chart before taking a look at some of the other types.

Adding a set of data

1. With the chart still selected, choose Ranges from the Chart menu to display this dialog box:

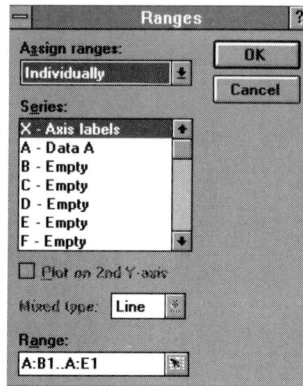

2. In the Series list box, click B - Empty. In the Range edit box, type *B9..E9*—the range containing the net income amounts—and click OK. 1-2-3 adds a second group of bars to the chart:

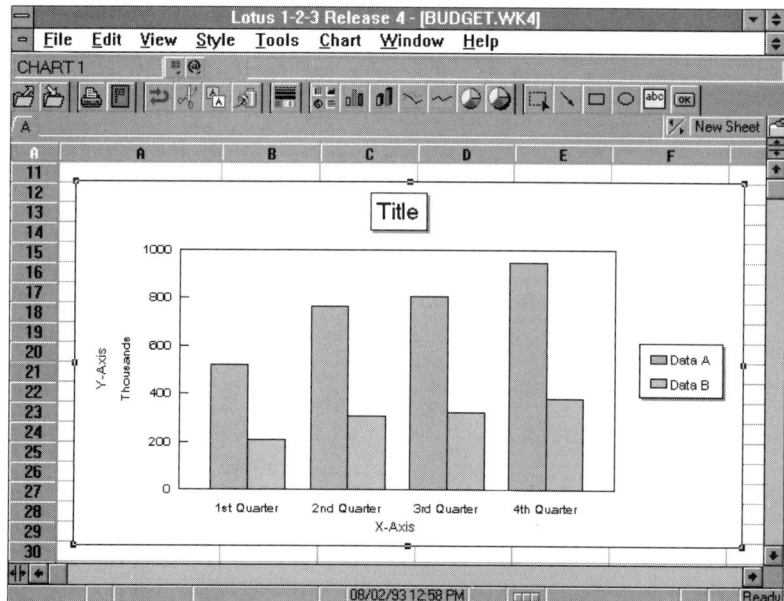

You can now compare sales with after-expenses income for each of the four quarters. Let's see what this data looks like in some other chart types:

3. Click the Line-Chart icon. Sales and net income are now represented as two separate lines on the chart:

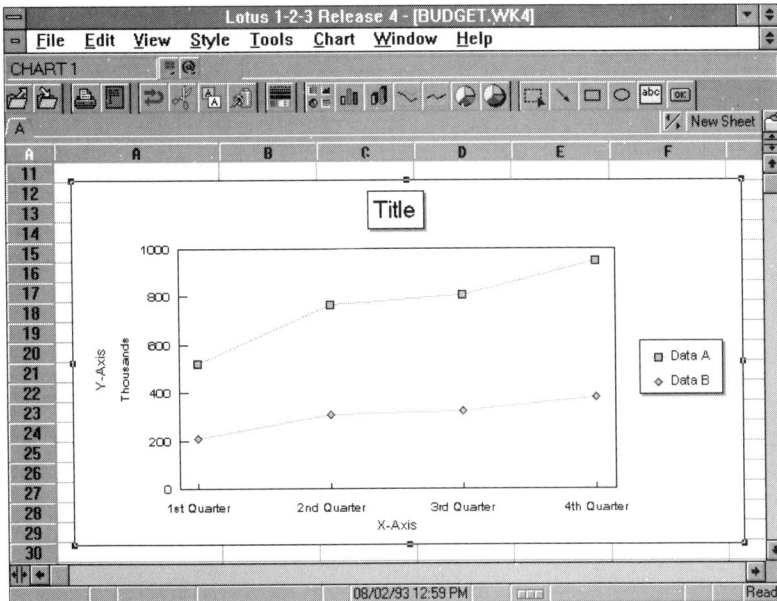

4. Click the 3D-Pie-Chart icon. Now the four quarters of sales data are represented as colored wedges in a circular pie with the illusion of three dimensions. You no longer see the net income data because a pie chart can display only one set of data.

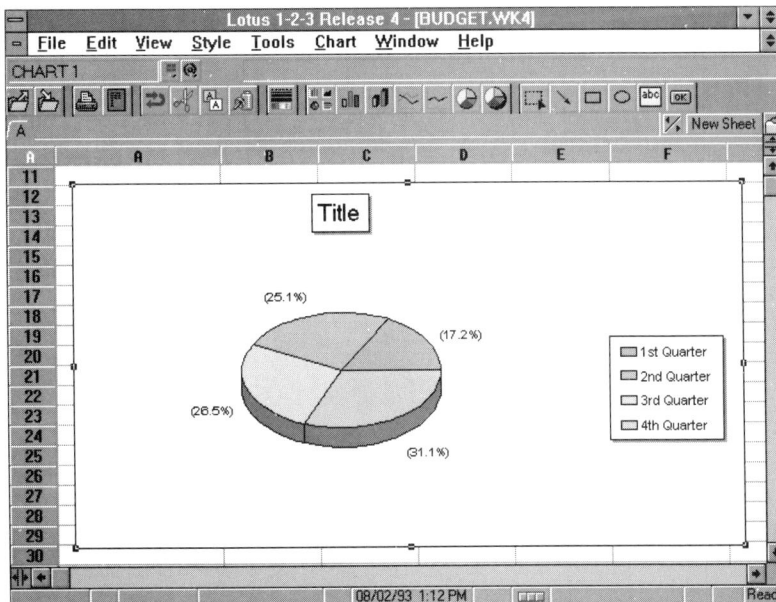

Preferred format

By default, 1-2-3 creates charts in what is called the *preferred format*. When you first start 1-2-3, the Preferred format is a plain bar chart. To change the Preferred format, start by creating a chart with the type, style, and grid settings you like. Then with the chart selected, choose the Set Preferred command from the Chart menu. Any new chart you create will then be in this format. The preferred format remains in effect until you change it.

5. Finally, click the 3D-Bar-Chart icon. The resulting chart displays vertical bars with the illusion of three dimensions:

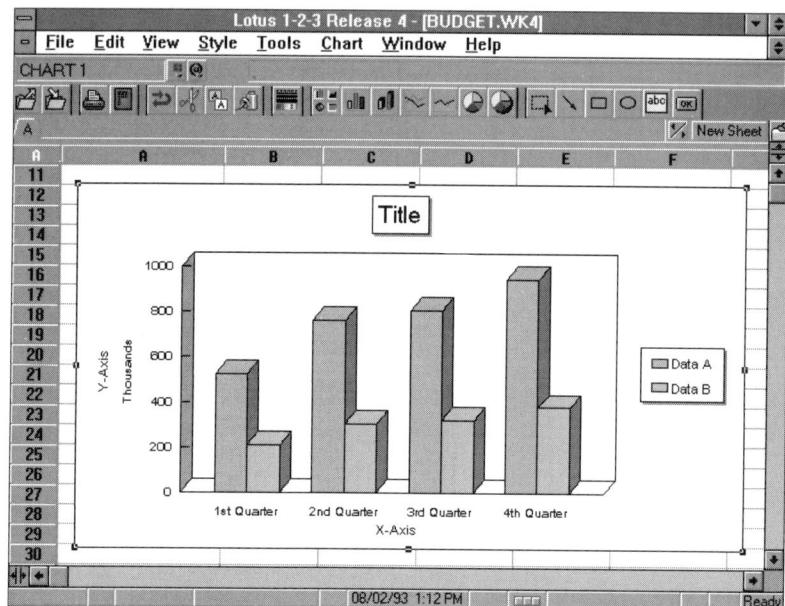

6. Click the other chart icons to get an idea of what's available. Finish up with a simple two-dimensional bar chart.

Using the Chart Type Command

Suppose you want to convert the current chart into a stacked bar chart in which sales and net income are represented in a single column and the values displayed in a table. To switch to this chart type, you must use the Type command on the Chart menu. Follow these steps:

1. Choose Type from the Chart menu to display this dialog box:

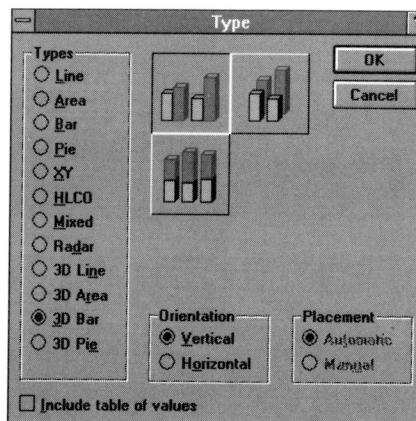

The Types section contains option buttons for all the chart types available in 1-2-3. Icons represent the variations available for the selected chart type. As you can see, the 3D Bar type has three variations—the simple bar chart, the perspective bar chart, and the stacked bar chart.

2. Before you make selections for the current chart, explore the variations available for some of the other types of charts. For example, click the Line, Area, Bar, and Pie options in the Types section, and then examine the variation icons. As you can see, 1-2-3 offers a rich variety of formats.

3. With 3D Bar selected in the Types section, click the stacked bar icon.

4. Click the Include Table Of Values check box at the bottom of the dialog box to tell 1-2-3 to incorporate the original worksheet data into the chart display.

Adding a table of data values

5. Click OK. Here are the results:

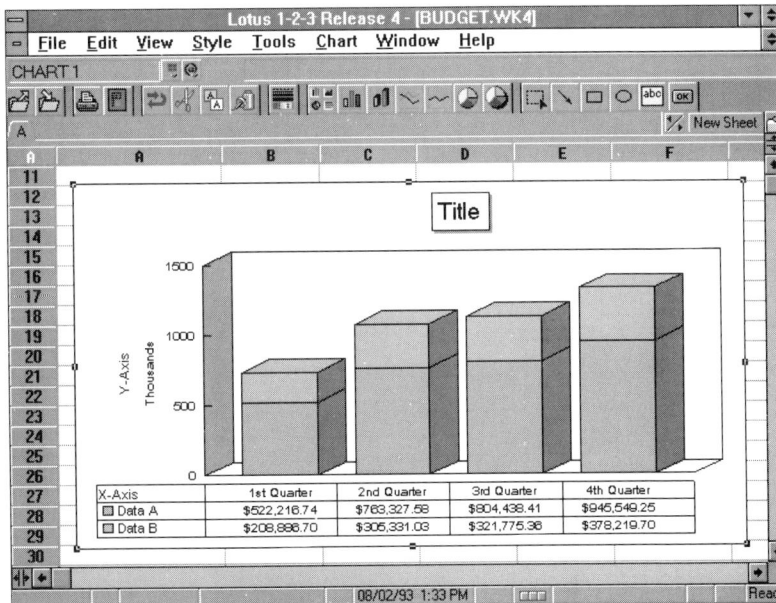

6. This effect is somewhat crowded, so restore the simple legend by double-clicking the chart to display the Type dialog box, deselecting Include Table Of Values.

Quick access to the Type dialog box

You might want to explore some of the other available chart types. In particular, try creating a mixed chart.

Customizing Charts

As we have said, 1-2-3 has a chart type for almost every occasion. But often you will want to refine the presentation of a chart by adding or changing specific elements. For this purpose, 1-2-3 provides a wealth of options you can use to customize your charts. We will review some of these options and make changes to our chart by adding titles, modifying legends, and changing grid lines. These elements increase almost any chart's clarity and persuasiveness.

Quick menus exist for almost every conceivable chart element. You might want to get a feel for the range of customization possibilities by right-clicking various chart elements (grid lines, axes, series, and so on) to open their shortcut menus. When you've finished experimenting on your own, we'll show you how to add a title to the chart currently on your screen.

Adding and Formatting Text

As you've seen, 1-2-3 automatically adds a Title box to the chart as a placeholder for your own title. To dress up the chart, you can customize this title, and you can add a subtitle and explanatory notes. (Titles appear at the top of the chart; notes appear at the bottom.) You can also customize the axis labels. All the fonts and attributes available for worksheet entries are available for chart text, so you can format the text any way you want. Follow these steps to add your own title to the chart:

Quick access to dialog boxes

You can double-click any chart element to display the main dialog box for that element. For example, double-clicking the y-axis displays the Y-Axis dialog box.

1. With the chart selected, right-click the Title box at the top of the chart and choose Headings to display this dialog box:

As you can see, you can create two titles and two notes.

2. In the Title section, type *1993 Budget* in the Line 1 edit box and *Sales and Net Income* in the Line 2 edit box and then click OK. On the chart, 1-2-3 replaces Title with the new heading.

Customizing the title

3. Right-click 1993 Budget in the chart to display the chart text quick menu. Then choose Fonts & Attributes to display this dialog box:

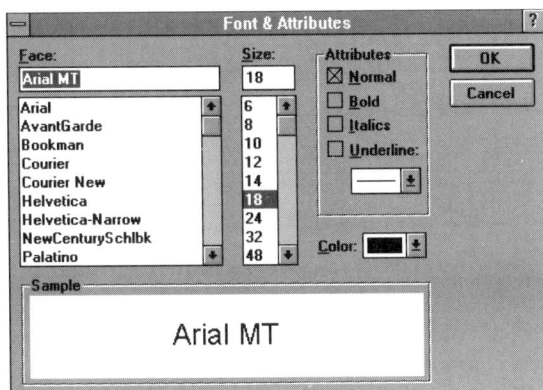

4. Select Times New Roman from the Face list box, leave the size as it is, click Bold and Italics in the Attributes section, and click OK.

   Now let's change the default axis labels to something more meaningful:

1. Choose Axis and then X-Axis from the Chart menu to display this dialog box:

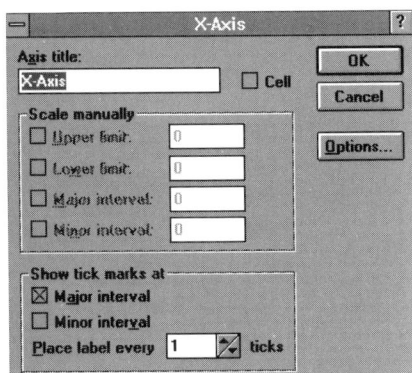

Axis numeric format

To change the format for the numbers on an axis, right-click an axis number and choose Number Format from the quick menu to display the Number Format dialog box. (You can also click the number format selector on the status bar.) Select the format you want for the axis numbers and then click OK.

2. Type *Quarters* in the Axis Title edit box and click OK.

3. Choose Axis and then Y-Axis from the Chart menu, type *Dollars* in the Axis Title edit box, and click OK.

4. Right-click the Quarters label, choose Font & Attributes, and format the label in 14-point Times New Roman bold. Then repeat this step for the Dollars label. Here are the results of all your formatting:

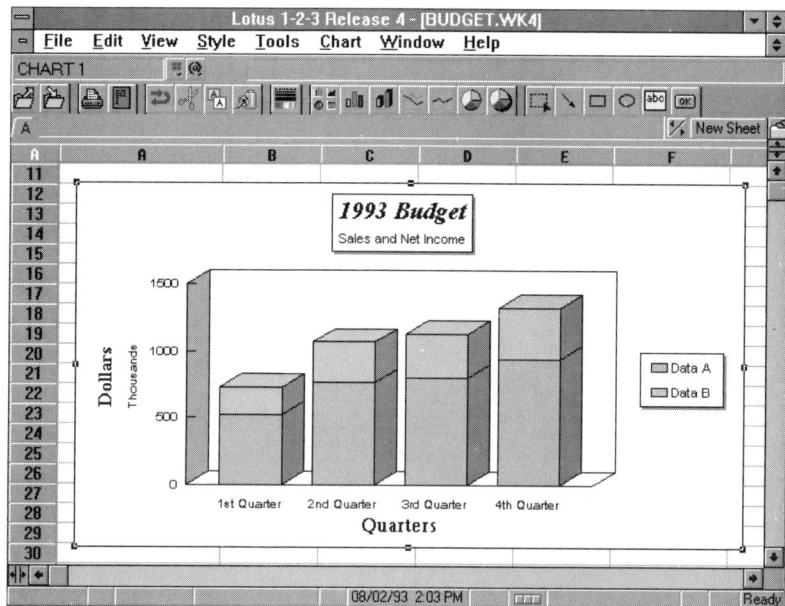

Modifying Legends

Axis settings

You can use the Axis command to change the scaling and tick marks on either axis. Select the axis you want to format, choose Axis from the Chart menu, and then choose Y-Axis or X-Axis from the Axis cascade menu. Then make your changes in the Scale Manually and Show Tick Marks At sections of the Axis dialog box.

Because you didn't select the labels in column A when you selected the data range you wanted 1-2-3 to plot, the labels in the legend are generic and meaningless, telling you only the order in which you plotted the two sets of data. Follow these steps to modify the legend:

1. Right-click the legend and choose Legend to display the Legend dialog box:

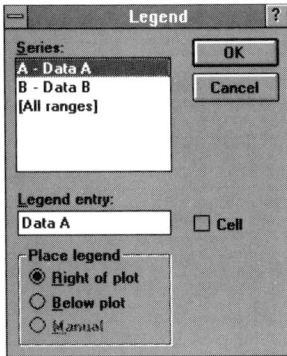

The current labels of the data ranges appear in the Series list box, and the highlighted label, Data A, appears in the Legend Entry edit box.

2. Click the Cell check box to tell 1-2-3 you want to use the contents of a cell on the worksheet for this legend entry, and then type *A2* in the Legend Entry edit box.

3. Select Data B in the Series list box and repeat step 2, replacing Data B in the Legend Entry edit box with A9.

4. In the Place Legend section, select Below Plot to tell 1-2-3 to move the legend below the chart. Click OK to see these results:

Positioning the legend

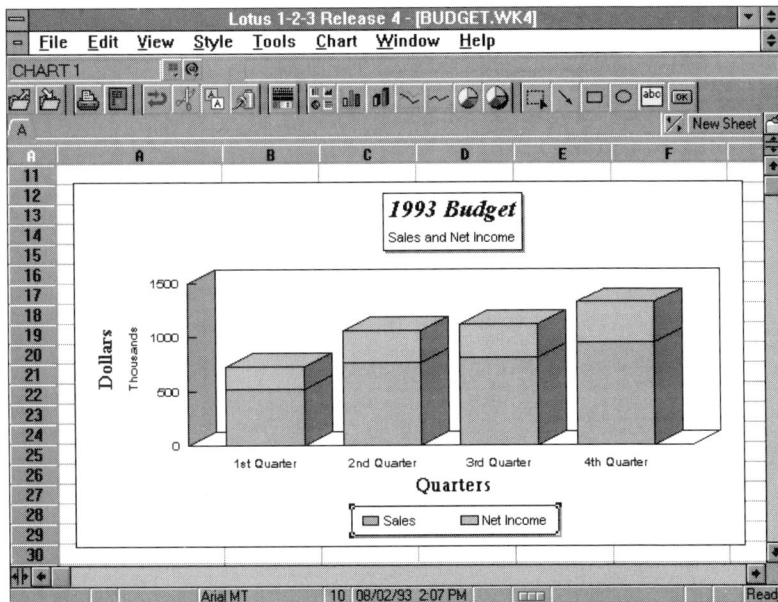

Adding a Designer Frame

The Lines & Color command allows you to choose colors, patterns, and line widths for different aspects of your chart (and your worksheets—see page 134). When the entire chart is selected, the command also includes frame selections. Here's how to change the chart's frame:

1. Right-click the background of the chart near the outer border and choose Lines & Color from the quick menu to display this dialog box:

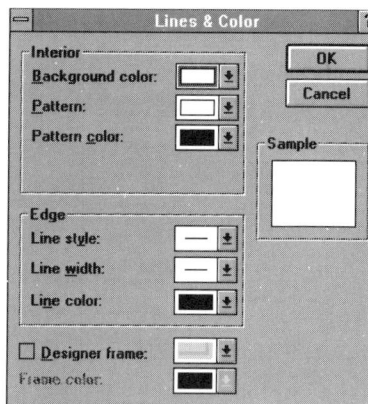

2. Click the down arrow at the right end of the Designer Frame edit box, select a frame, and click OK.

You can also use this dialog box to give the chart's background a color or pattern.

Adding Grid Lines

When grid lines would make it easier to make sense of plotted data, you can easily add them to your charts. You can add lines for major or minor intervals on either or both axes. Let's add grid lines to the 1993 Budget chart:

1. Right-click an empty spot inside the "box" containing the chart's columns and choose Grids from the quick menu to display this dialog box:

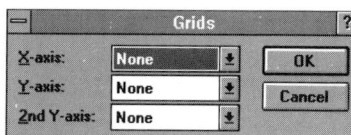

Drawing

You can use the drawing icons on the Chart and Default Sheet SmartIcon palettes to add objects such as lines and circles to your documents. After clicking one of these SmartIcons, you use the mouse to specify the new object's size and position:

Arrow draws a forward pointing arrow.
Ellipse draws an ellipse or circle.
Rectangle draws a rectangle or square.

You can also draw objects on your worksheets and charts by choosing Draw and then a cascade menu command from the Tools menu.

2. From the X-Axis drop-down list box, select Minor Interval. Repeat this step for the y-axis and then click OK. The chart now looks like this:

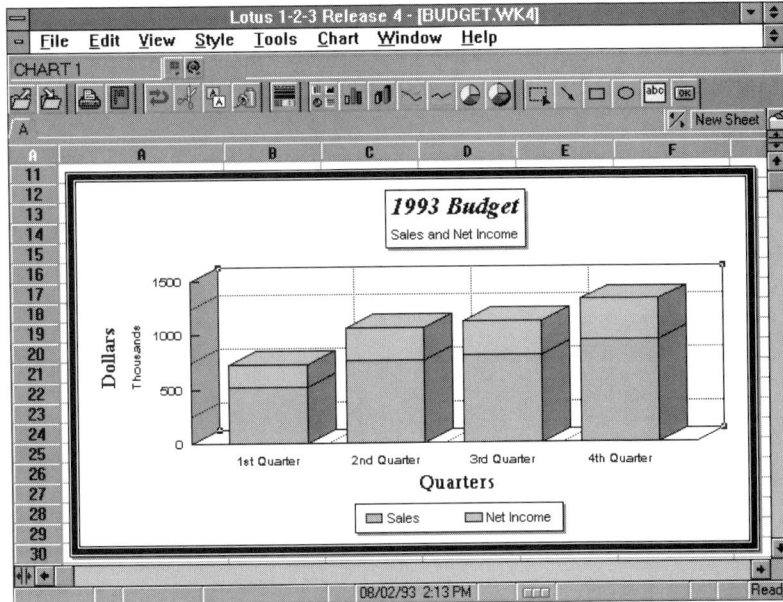

3. Save your chart before moving on.

We won't take our customization experiments any further but will leave you to explore on your own. When you're ready, rejoin us to print your chart.

Printing and Previewing Charts

Printing and previewing charts is much like printing and previewing worksheets. You can print and preview the worksheet data and chart together or just the chart. (A chart document can never be more than one page, so the Next and Previous buttons are not available when you preview just the chart.) Follow these steps to print your chart:

1. Press Home, and then click the Preview icon. When the Print Preview dialog box appears, select the Current Worksheet option and click OK. Your screen now looks as shown on the next page.

Previewing the data and the chart

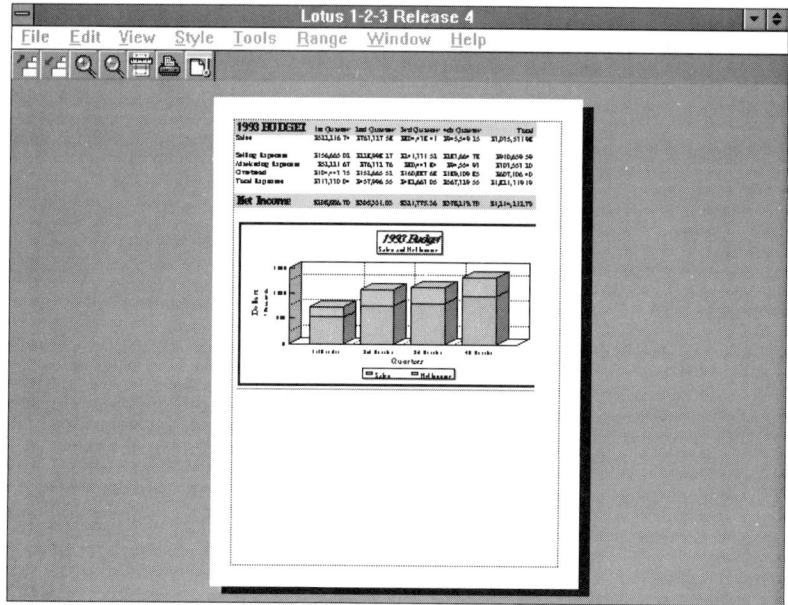

If you wanted to print the worksheet and the chart neatly on one page, you would need to adjust the width of the chart to align with the right edge of the Total column.

2. Click the Close icon to return to the worksheet.

Previewing the chart only

3. Next select the chart and click the Preview icon again. Click OK to accept the Selected Chart option in the Print Preview dialog box. Print Preview now shows only the chart.

4. Click the Page Setup icon to display this dialog box:

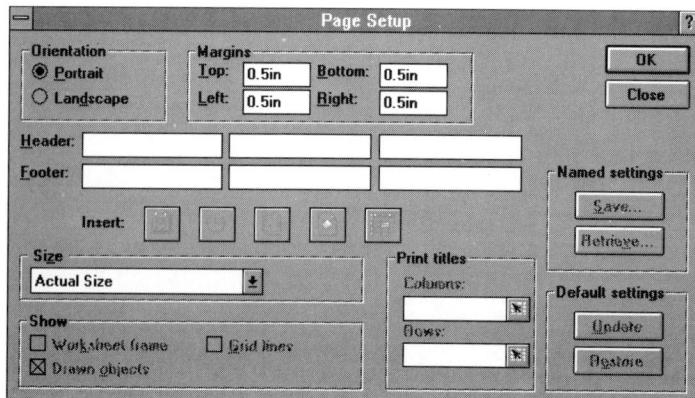

5. In the Orientation section, select Landscape.

6. Click the down arrow at the right end of the Size edit box. The options on the drop-down list allow you to specify whether the chart should be printed the same size as it appears on the screen (Actual Size), enlarged proportionally until it fits within the specified page margins (Fill Page But Keep Proportions), or enlarged to fit without regard to width:height ratios (Fill Page). Select Fill Page But Keep Proportions and click OK. The preview window now looks like this:

Sizing for printing

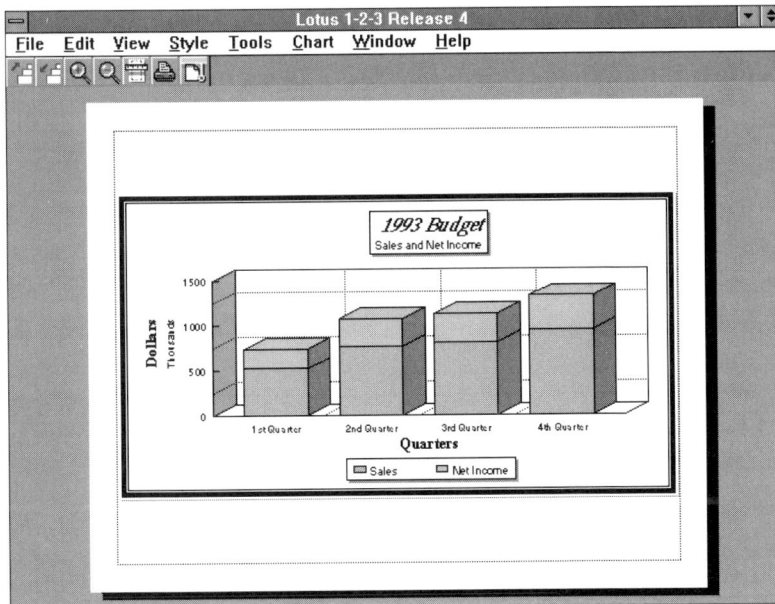

If you want, you can now click the Print icon to create a paper copy of your chart.

1-2-3's charting features make creating charts easy, and with the quick menus, adding special touches is a snap. Be creative and have fun!

Multiple Worksheets, Versions, and Scenarios

What you will learn

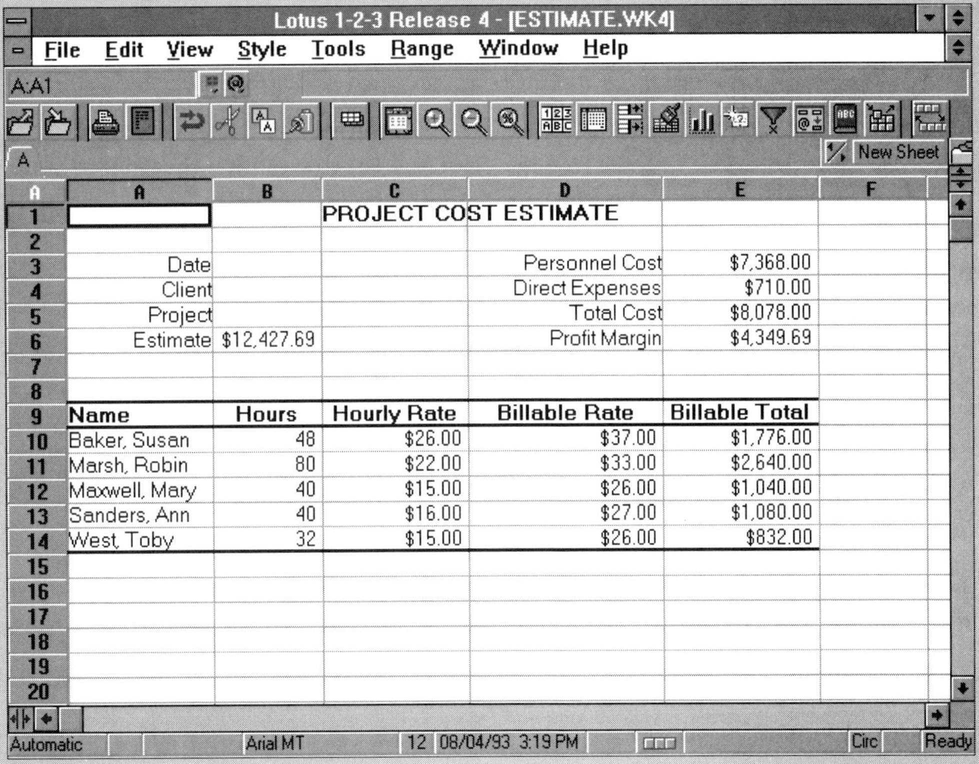

File   Edit   View   Style   Tools   Range   Window   Help

A:A1

A

New Sheet

	A	B	C	D	E	F
1			PROJECT COST ESTIMATE			
2						
3	Date			Personnel Cost	$7,368.00	
4	Client			Direct Expenses	$710.00	
5	Project			Total Cost	$8,078.00	
6	Estimate	$12,427.69		Profit Margin	$4,349.69	
7						
8						
9	Name	Hours	Hourly Rate	Billable Rate	Billable Total	
10	Baker, Susan	48	$26.00	$37.00	$1,776.00	
11	Marsh, Robin	80	$22.00	$33.00	$2,640.00	
12	Maxwell, Mary	40	$15.00	$26.00	$1,040.00	
13	Sanders, Ann	40	$16.00	$27.00	$1,080.00	
14	West, Toby	32	$15.00	$26.00	$832.00	
15						
16						
17						
18						
19						
20						

Automatic   Arial MT   12   08/04/93 3:19 PM   Circ   Ready

In this chapter, we tackle a more ambitious set of worksheets. First we create tables of employee information and overhead costs. Then we create a worksheet that estimates project costs by "looking up" hourly rates in one of the tables. Next, we cover a technique called *iteration*, which enables 1-2-3 to resolve circular calculations. Finally, we use 1-2-3's version management feature to create multiple versions of our cost sheet to reflect different scenarios.

In our example, we create only employee information and overhead tables, because the primary cost involved in the sample project estimate is for people's time. However, you can easily adapt the project cost estimate worksheet to incorporate marketing expenses or materials information. For example, if you manage a construction business that specializes in bathroom and kitchen remodeling, you can create a table with up-to-date prices for fixtures, plumbing supplies, cabinets, tile, and so on, in addition to the employee information and overhead tables. Even if you are a one-person operation with no employees, you can still adapt the worksheet to make sure that you include overhead and marketing costs in your project estimates.

This chapter differs from previous chapters in that we don't bog down the instructions with information you already know. For example, we might show you a worksheet and ask you to create it, without always telling you step by step what to enter, how to apply formats and styles, and how to adjust column widths. We leave it up to you to create the worksheet using the illustration as a guide. Similarly, we might tell you to create a formula, assuming that you know how to enter a function in a cell and how to click cells to use their references as arguments.

Multiple sheets vs. multiple worksheets

In previous chapters, we organized information in multiple sheets (named A, B, C, and so on) saved within a single file. In this chapter, we'll work with three different worksheet files, and we'll show you how to create links between them.

Creating the Supporting Tables

The logical way to begin this example is to enter the data needed for the two supporting tables. There's nothing complicated about these tables; we've stripped them down so that you don't have to type any extraneous information. The few calculations involved have been greatly simplified and do not reflect the gyrations accountants would go through to ensure to-the-penny accuracy. So instead of describing step by step how to create these tables, we'll simply show them to you and, after discussing the few formulas and cell and range names involved, let you create them on your own.

1. In a blank worksheet, create the table of employee information shown below, and then save it as EMPLOYEE.WK4:

The employee
information table

```
Lotus 1-2-3 Release 4 - [EMPLOYEE.WK4]
File   Edit   View   Style   Tools   Range   Window   Help
A1                                               New Sheet
```

	A	B	C	D	E	F	G
1		EMPLOYEE INFORMATION					
2							
3	Name	Salary	Salary/Hour	Emp. Costs	Costs/Hour	Hourly Rate	Billable
4	Baker, Susan	32000					y
5	Cash, John	22000					y
6	Collins, Peter	40000					y
7	Dixon, Sally	50000					
8	Marsh, Robin	27000					y
9	Maxwell, Mary	18000					y
10	Parkins, Dee	22000					
11	Sanders, Ann	20000					y
12	Sexton, Alex	24000					y
13	West, Toby	19000					y
14							
15							
16							
17							
18							
19							
20							

```
Automatic        Arial MT        12  08/04/93  1:23 PM                    Ready
```

2. In row 4, enter these formulas:

C4 +B4/50/30
Annual salary divided by 50 weeks (allowing 2 weeks for vacation), divided by 30 billable hours per week (allowing 2 hours per day of non-billable time)

D4 +B4*.22
Employer contributions to social security and benefits estimated at 22 percent of annual salary

Ascending order

You can list employees in the employee information table in any order, but before 1-2-3 can use the table to look up information, you must sort it in ascending order. 1-2-3 cannot look up information in randomly ordered tables or in tables in descending order. Select the range, and choose the Sort command from the Range menu to sort the table.

E4	+D4/52/30
	Employer contributions to social security and benefits divided by 52 weeks divided by 30 hours per week

The @ROUND function

F4	@ROUND(C4+E4,0)
	Salary per hour plus benefits per hour, rounded to a whole number (0 decimal places)

3. After entering the formulas in row 4, select C4..F13 and use the Copy Down command on the quick menu to copy the row 4 formulas to rows 5 through 13.

Quick number formats

4. Use the status bar's number format and decimal place selectors to apply the Comma 0-decimal format to columns B and D, the Fixed 2-decimal format to columns C and E, and the Fixed 0-decimal format to column F. Then change the column width as needed to make the table more readable.

5. Choose Name from the Range menu to assign the name BILLABLE to cells G4:G14 and the name EMP_RATE to cells A4:F14. (See page 41 for information about how to assign range names.) We'll use these names in future formulas to create links between this and other worksheets. Press Home and save your work. Here is the completed table:

Extending named ranges

It is a good idea to include a blank row or column at the end of the range when assigning range names. If you need to add employees to the EMPLOYEE worksheet, for example, you can select the blank row below the last entry and choose the Insert command from the Edit menu to extend the range with the name BILLABLE.

	A	B	C	D	E	F	G
1		EMPLOYEE INFORMATION					
3	Name	Salary	Salary/Hour	Emp. Costs	Costs/Hour	Hourly Rate	Billable
4	Baker, Susan	32,000	21.33	7,040	4.51	26	y
5	Cash, John	22,000	14.67	4,840	3.10	18	y
6	Collins, Peter	40,000	26.67	8,800	5.64	32	y
7	Dixon, Sally	50,000	33.33	11,000	7.05	40	
8	Marsh, Robin	27,000	18.00	5,940	3.81	22	y
9	Maxwell, Mary	18,000	12.00	3,960	2.54	15	y
10	Parkins, Dee	22,000	14.67	4,840	3.10	18	
11	Sanders, Ann	20,000	13.33	4,400	2.82	16	y
12	Sexton, Alex	24,000	16.00	5,280	3.38	19	y
13	West, Toby	19,000	12.67	4,180	2.68	15	y

That's it for the employee information table. Let's move on to the overhead table:

1. Choose New from the File menu to open a new worksheet and save the blank worksheet as OVERHEAD.WK4. Then create the first part of the table as shown below.

The overhead table

```
Lotus 1-2-3 Release 4 - [OVERHEAD.WK4]
File  Edit  View  Style  Tools  Range  Window  Help
A:A3              @        'Name
                                              New Sheet
      A            B        C          D          E        F         G
1              OVERHEAD (FIXED) COSTS
2
3  Name         Salary   Salary/Hour  Emp. Costs Costs/Hour Hourly Rate
4  Dixon, Sally  50,000
5  Parkins, Dee  22,000
6
7
8  Expenses     Budget
9  Rent         24,000
10 Insurance     1,350
11 Equipment    10,000
12 Supplies      7,000
13
14 Total
15
16
17
18
19
20
Automatic          Arial MT      12  08/04/93  1:53 PM              Ready
```

2. Sally Dixon and Dee Parkins are administrative employees who do not directly generate income for the company, so we need to include their salaries and benefits in this overhead calculation. You can copy the entries from row 4 of the EMPLOYEE worksheet using the Copy and Paste icons, or you can enter them from scratch. If you choose to enter them from scratch, here are the formulas to use in row 4:

C4   +B4/50/30 (with Fixed 2-decimal format)
D4   +B4*.22 (with Comma 0-decimal format)
E4   +D4/52/30 (with Fixed 2-decimal format)
F4   @ROUND(C4+E4,0) (with Fixed 0-decimal format)

3. After completing the formulas in row 4, copy them to row 5.

4. Next enter *Expenses/Hour* in cell C14 and *Total Billable Overhead/Hour* in cell C16, and make the labels bold.

Justifying within a range

5. Select C14..E16, and choose Alignment from the Style menu. 1-2-3 displays this dialog box:

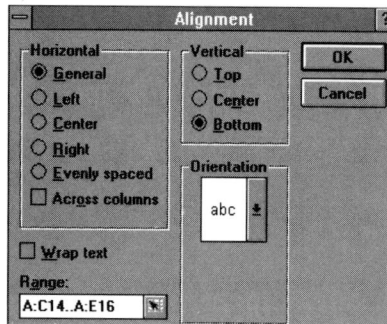

6. In the Horizontal section, select Right and click the Across Columns check box. Click OK. 1-2-3 right-justifies the two labels within the range you have selected, and the worksheet now looks like this:

7. Now enter and format these formulas in the designated cells:

B14	@SUM(B9..B13)
F14	@ROUND(B14/52/30,0)
F16	@SUM(F4..F14)

We must bill 30 hours each week at the rate in F16 to cover overhead costs. We cannot bill overhead to a client directly, so we must increase the hourly rate of employees with billable hours by a prorated amount to ensure that overhead is included in project estimates. To calculate the prorated overhead amount, we need to divide the total billable rate per hour in cell F16 by the number of employees who generate income. We can glance at the employee information worksheet and know that this value is 8, but what if the company had many employees? We need to link the employee information worksheet and the overhead worksheet so that 1-2-3 can supply this number for us.

We establish the link by entering a formula in one worksheet that contains a reference to a cell or range in the other worksheet. This "link" formula includes a reference to the linked worksheet—its filename and directory path—along with a reference to the target cell or range. If you are systematic about defining appropriate range names in worksheets you want to link, 1-2-3 provides you with a very simple technique for creating a link to another file while you are writing a formula: You simply press the F3 key to display the Range Names dialog box and select the file reference from the list in this box. You'll have a chance to practice this technique in the next section.

Linking worksheets

Counting Entries

We can tell 1-2-3 to count the number of employees who have a *y* entry in the Billable column of EMPLOYEE.WK4 by using the @COUNT function. This function scans the range specified as its argument and counts the number of nonblank cells in the range. Here's how to use @COUNT in the formula that calculates the overhead allocation:

The @COUNT function

1. In cell C17 of OVERHEAD.WK4, type *Prorated Overhead/ Hour*, and press Enter. Next use the Alignment command on the Style menu to right-justify this label over the range C17..E17, just as you did for the two labels above it. Then make the label bold.

2. We want the prorated amount to be in whole dollars, so we need to nest the prorated calculation in an @ROUND function. In cell F17, type the following:

@ROUND(F16/@COUNT(

3. To divide the hourly overhead in cell F16 by the number of employees whose hours are billable, you must now insert a reference to the range that you defined as BILLABLE in the EMPLOYEE.WK4 worksheet. Press the F3 function key to display this Range Names dialog box:

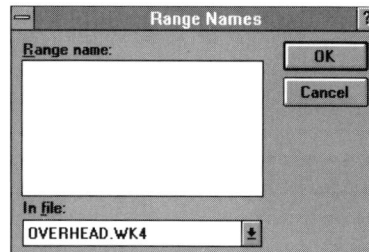

File references

4. Click the down arrow at the right end of the In File edit box and select the EMPLOYEE worksheet. Then select BILL-ABLE from the Range Name edit box and click OK. In response, 1-2-3 inserts a file reference to the range named BILLABLE, thereby linking the two worksheets. As you can see, 1-2-3 encloses a reference to a file in double angle brackets (<< and >>).

5. Next, type a) to close the @COUNT function. Then type a comma, a zero, and a final) to close the @ROUND function. Finally, press Enter.

6. Click the contents box at the top of the screen and check that it contains the following formula.

@ROUND(F16/@COUNT(<<C:\123R4W\SAMPLE\
    EMPLOYEE. WK4>>BILLABLE),0)

The file reference includes the complete directory path of the EMPLOYEE.WK4 file; this path reflects the location of the file and will be displayed differently if you have saved your file in a directory other than C:\123R4W\SAMPLE.

7. Make any necessary corrections and then press Enter. 1-2-3 calculates the formula and enters the value 11 in cell F17:

Flexible formulas

Keep in mind that using names in formulas makes your worksheets much more flexible than using cell references. If the information referenced in a formula moves because of changes you make to a worksheet, 1-2-3 adjusts the definition of the name so that the formula can continue to access the correct information.

Lotus 1-2-3 Release 4 - [OVERHEAD.WK4]

File Edit View Style Tools Range Window Help

A:F17 @ROUND(F16/@COUNT(<<C:\123R4W\SAMPLE\EMPLOYEE.WK4>>B|

	A	B	C	D	E	F	G
1		OVERHEAD (FIXED) COSTS					
2							
3	Name	Salary	Salary/Hour	Emp. Costs	Costs/Hour	Hourly Rate	
4	Dixon, Sally	50,000	33.33	11,000	7.05	40	
5	Parkins, Dee	22,000	14.67	4,840	3.10	18	
6							
7							
8	Expenses	Budget					
9	Rent	24,000					
10	Insurance	1,350					
11	Equipment	10,000					
12	Supplies	7,000					
13							
14	Total	42,350			Expenses/Hour	27	
15							
16				Total Billable Overhead/Hour		85	
17				Prorated Overhead/Hour		11	

8. Assign the name OVER_RATE to cell F17.

Creating the Estimate Worksheet

With the two tables in place, we're ready to create the worksheet for estimating project costs. We'll put the basic structure of the worksheet in place first, and then we'll fill in the formulas necessary for the calculations.

1. Choose New from the File menu to open another new worksheet. Save this file as ESTIMATE.WK4. Then create the top area of the worksheet, as shown here:

The estimate worksheet

Lotus 1-2-3 Release 4 - [ESTIMATE.WK4]

File Edit View Style Tools Range Window Help

A:A1

	A	B	C	D	E	F	G
1			PROJECT COST ESTIMATE				
2							
3	Date			Personnel Cost			
4	Client			Direct Expenses			
5	Project			Total Cost			
6	Estimate			Profit Margin			

Smart links

Once you have entered a file reference to establish a link between two worksheets, 1-2-3 will be able to locate the information it needs whether or not the referenced worksheet is open.

2. Next, enter the headings in row 9 for the table where we'll calculate the personnel costs of the project and enter the

employee names and the number of hours you anticipate each
will need to work on this project, as shown here:

Lotus 1-2-3 Release 4 - [ESTIMATE.WK4]

A:B15

	A	B	C	D	E	F
1			PROJECT COST ESTIMATE			
2						
3	Date			Personnel Cost		
4	Client			Direct Expenses		
5	Project			Total Cost		
6	Estimate			Profit Margin		
7						
8						
9	Name	Hours	Hourly Rate	Billable Rate	Billable Total	
10	Baker, Susan	48				
11	Marsh, Robin	80				
12	Maxwell, Mary	40				
13	Sanders, Ann	40				
14	West, Toby	32				
15						

**Drawing lines above
and below cells**

3. Draw a thick line above and below the new headings by first
selecting the range A9..E9 and then choosing Lines & Color
from the Style menu to display the Lines & Color dialog box:

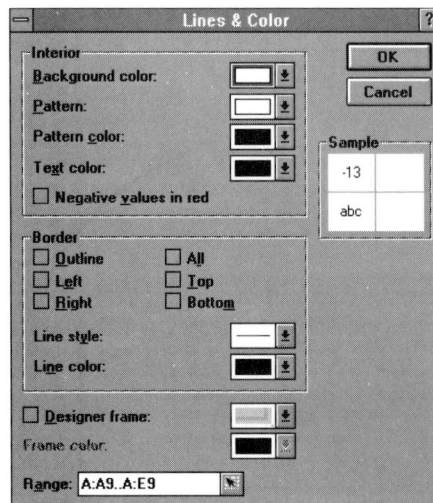

Lines & Color

Interior
Background color:
Pattern:
Pattern color:
Text color:
☐ Negative values in red

Sample
-13
abc

OK
Cancel

Border
☐ Outline   ☐ All
☐ Left   ☐ Top
☐ Right   ☐ Bottom

Line style:
Line color:

☐ Designer frame:
Frame color:

Range: A:A9..A:E9

4. Click the Top check box in the Border section. Then click the
down arrow at the right end of the Line Style edit box and
select the third line in the list box. Then click the Bottom
check box. The boxes to the right display the selected thick
line. Click OK.

5. Finally, draw a line below the last row of entries by selecting
A15..E15, choosing Lines & Color from the Style menu,

clicking the Top check box, selecting the third line from the Line Style drop-down list, and clicking OK. The worksheet now looks like this:

	A	B	C	D	E	F
1			PROJECT COST ESTIMATE			
2						
3	Date			Personnel Cost		
4	Client			Direct Expenses		
5	Project			Total Cost		
6	Estimate			Profit Margin		
7						
8						
9	Name	Hours	Hourly Rate	Billable Rate	Billable Total	
10	Baker, Susan	48				
11	Marsh, Robin	80				
12	Maxwell, Mary	40				
13	Sanders, Ann	40				
14	West, Toby	32				
15						

So far, everything has been pretty straightforward and has provided you with nothing more challenging than an opportunity to practice skills you learned in other chapters. Now we need to introduce the 1-2-3 function that will enable you to use one of the tables you created earlier to fill in the information needed for this worksheet.

Looking Up Information

1-2-3 has a variety of functions you can use in formulas to look up information in worksheet tables. Among them are @VLOOKUP (which is for vertically oriented tables), and @HLOOKUP (which is for horizontally oriented tables). Here, we'll show you how to use @VLOOKUP.

The @VLOOKUP function

1-2-3 needs three pieces of information to carry out the @VLOOKUP function: the entry you want it to look up, the range of the lookup table, and the column number in the table from which the function should copy a value. To search for a label in the lookup table, you supply these three pieces of information in this way:

Lookup table

@VLOOKUP(*label,table,column*)

1-2-3 searches down the leftmost column of the lookup table for the row that contains the label you supply as the first argument. Then, if 1-2-3 finds the label, the @VLOOKUP function returns the value from the intersection of the same row and the column you specify as the third argument. (You identify a column in the lookup table as a value from 0 up to *n*–1, where *n* is the number of columns in the table. This value is known as the column's *offset value*.) For example, to look up the hourly rate for John Cash in the employee information table, you could move to the EMPLOYEE worksheet and enter the following function, say in cell A19:

@VLOOKUP("Cash, John",A4..G13,5)

1-2-3 scans the leftmost column—column A—for the text entry *Cash, John*. When it finds the entry it's looking for in cell A5, it looks across the same row to the fifth column—column F—and copies the value 18 from cell F5 to cell A19.

Let's see how to put the @VLOOKUP function to work in the project cost estimate worksheet:

1. Select cell C10 of ESTIMATE.WK4, click the number format selector on the status bar, and choose Currency. Then enter the beginning of the formula as

@VLOOKUP(A10,

2. Press the F3 key. In the Range Names dialog box, click the down arrow at the right end of the In File edit box and select EMPLOYEE.WK4 from the list box. Then double-click the range name EMP_RATE. 1-2-3 inserts a reference to this range in the formula you are building.

Converting relative to absolute

3. Press the F4 key to tell 1-2-3 to change the most recently entered reference from relative to absolute. To indicate that the reference is now absolute, 1-2-3 inserts a dollar sign before the range name: $EMP_RATE. This step is necessary because you are going to copy the formula down column C, and you want the reference to the lookup table to remain unchanged in each copy.

4. Type a comma. Then type *5* and a close) to finish the formula. Press Enter. 1-2-3 looks up the value in cell A10 (*Baker, Susan*) in the table called EMP_RATE in EMPLOYEE.WK4 and enters the corresponding hourly rate, as shown here:

5. Now select C10..C14 in the ESTIMATE worksheet, right-click the range, and choose Copy Down from the quick menu to enter equivalent formulas that look up the hourly rates for the other people who will be involved in the project. When you complete this copy operation, examine the new formulas, and notice that the absolute reference to the lookup table ($EMP_RATE) was copied unchanged to each one.

Completing the Estimate

Well, the hard part is over. A few simple calculations, and you'll be ready to prepare an estimate for your client.

1. In the ESTIMATE worksheet, enter the following formulas in the indicated cells, and then apply the Currency format to the results:

D10 +C10+<<C:\123R4W\SAMPLE\OVERHEAD. WK4>> $OVER_RATE

E10 +B10*D10

Notice that the formula in cell D10 contains an absolute reference to the range OVER_RATE. Again you use the F3 key to select this range name from the Range Names dialog box, and then the F4 key to change it to an absolute reference.

2. Use the Copy Down command to copy the formulas to D11..D14 and E11..E14.

Now you can calculate total costs in the summary area at the top of the worksheet:

1. Make these entries in the indicated cells and apply the Currency format:

E3   @SUM(E10..E14)
E4   710
E5   +E3+E4

The entry in cell E4 is an estimate of charges that will be incurred for long-distance phone calls, delivery services, and other expenses attributable directly to the project. As you can see, this worksheet is almost complete:

Automatic calculation

By default, 1-2-3 immediately calculates a formula when you enter it and also recalculates any of the existing formulas in open worksheets that are affected by the new entry. While 1-2-3 performs this automatic calculation, it displays the word Calc in the status bar.

Projecting Profit Margin with Iteration

Probably the most difficult part of estimating a project is figuring out the profit margin. We now have a good idea what this project is going to cost. But suppose we need a margin of roughly 35 percent of the estimate total to be sure we make a profit. How do we calculate the actual profit margin when we don't yet know the estimate total, and how do we calculate the estimate total when we don't know the profit margin? We could go in circles forever.

Fortunately, we can have 1-2-3 go in circles for us. Using the iteration technique, we can force 1-2-3 to calculate the margin formula over and over until it can give us an answer. Follow these steps:

1. Select cell E6 in the ESTIMATE.WK4 worksheet, apply the Currency format, and enter this formula:

+.35*B6

2. Now select cell B6, apply the Currency format, and enter this formula:

@SUM(E5..E6)

The word Circ appears in the status bar at the bottom of the window. 1-2-3 displays this message because the formula in B6 contains a reference to cell E6, and the formula in E6 contains a reference to B6.

3. Double-click the word Circ. 1-2-3 moves the cell pointer to E6, the cell containing the formula that created the circular reference:

Resolving circular references

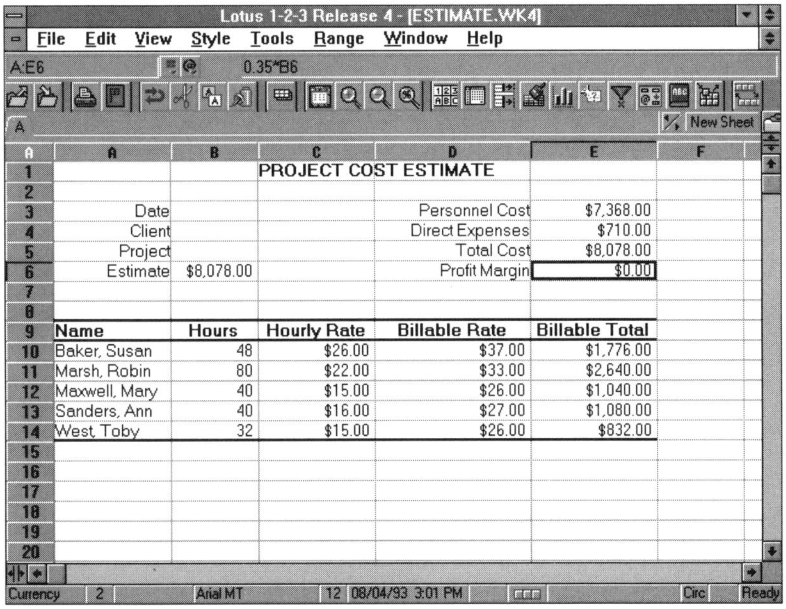

Manual calculation

To tell 1-2-3 to calculate open worksheets only when you press the F9 key, choose User Setup from the Tools menu, click Recalculation, and then select the Manual option. You might want to activate this option for large worksheets, where recalculating each formula can take some time.

On the worksheet, the value displayed in cell E6 is still $0.00. You now need to instruct 1-2-3 to calculate the formulas in E6 and B6 many times—in an iterative process—until a reasonable estimate is found for the profit margin. Here's how to force 1-2-3 to come up with an answer:

1. Choose User Setup from the Tools menu to display the User Setup dialog box and then click the Recalculation button to display this dialog box:

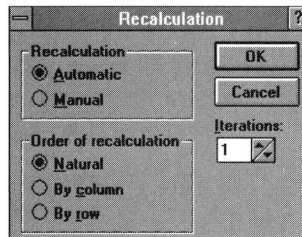

2. Type *50* in the Iterations edit box to tell 1-2-3 to perform the iterative calculation of the circular formulas 50 times, and then click OK twice.

The recalculation key

3. Press F9. 1-2-3 quickly recalculates the formulas, finally coming up with these results:

Order of recalculation

You can tell 1-2-3 to recalculate your worksheets in one of three ways. Choose User Setup from the Tools menu, click Recalculation, and then select Natural to tell 1-2-3 to calculate the current formula after recalculating the formulas it depends on; select By Column to tell 1-2-3 to move column by column, recalculating formulas as it goes; and select By Row to tell 1-2-3 to move row by row.

PROJECT COST ESTIMATE

	A	B	C	D	E	F
3	Date			Personnel Cost	$7,368.00	
4	Client			Direct Expenses	$710.00	
5	Project			Total Cost	$8,078.00	
6	Estimate	$12,427.69		Profit Margin	$4,349.69	
9	Name	Hours	Hourly Rate	Billable Rate	Billable Total	
10	Baker, Susan	48	$26.00	$37.00	$1,776.00	
11	Marsh, Robin	80	$22.00	$33.00	$2,640.00	
12	Maxwell, Mary	40	$15.00	$26.00	$1,040.00	
13	Sanders, Ann	40	$16.00	$27.00	$1,080.00	
14	West, Toby	32	$15.00	$26.00	$832.00	

By selecting the Iteration option, you tell 1-2-3 to keep re-calculating the formula, going in circles for 50 iterations. The result might not be exact, but in this situation, inaccuracies of less than a penny are not likely to cause concern.

Creating Multiple Versions and Scenarios

The completed project estimate worksheet shows current employee and overhead costs. What if we knew that our company would be moving into a new facility next year, and the overhead costs would increase? We can use 1-2-3's Version Manager to create multiple *versions* of the expense information and then build *scenarios* with these different versions so that we can analyze project costs before and after the move.

The Version Manager

To demonstrate some of the capabilities of the Version Manager, we'll assign the current nonemployee expenses of our overhead table to a version name, then create another version with future nonemployee expenses. Then we'll assign these versions to different scenario names and change the scenarios to see the effect on project costs.

Creating Versions

Let's start by designating the expenses range as a version:

1. Switch to the OVERHEAD worksheet, select A9..B13 and choose Version from the Range menu. 1-2-3 provides two version management dialog boxes: the Version Manager and the Version Manager Index. The Version Manager is convenient for working with a single version, and the Version Manager Index is useful for working with multiple versions and scenarios. Because we will create multiple versions of our expenses range, we'll use the Version Manager Index. If Version Manager is displayed in the title bar of your dialog box, click the To Index icon to display the Version Manager Index dialog box shown on the next page.

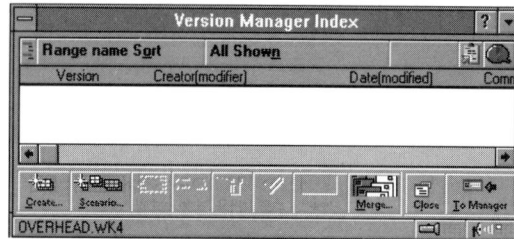

2. Click the Create button to display this dialog box:

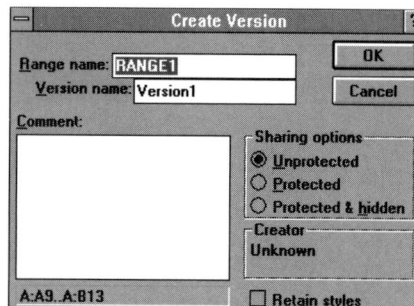

3. Type *EXPENSES* in the Range Name edit box. Then type *Current* in the Version Name edit box. Click the Retain Styles check box and then click OK once to create a version of the expenses range named Current, complete with formatting.

Now create a version of the expenses range named Future:

1. With the Version Manager Index still displayed, select cell B9, change the Rent amount to 28000, and press Down Arrow. Change the Insurance amount in B10 to 1600, press Down Arrow, and change the Equipment amount in B11 to 16000. 1-2-3 italicizes the Current entry in the Version Manager Index dialog box to show that the range has been modified since the last version update.

2. Click the Create button in the Version Manager Index dialog box. In the Create Version dialog box, leave the Range Name entry as EXPENSES and then type *Future* in the Version Name edit box. Click the Retain Styles check box and then click OK. Again, leave the Version Manager Index dialog box on your screen.

Updating version ranges

When you update data or styles in a version range, you must also update the version in the Version Manager Index dialog box to save the changes to the range. You select the version name from the Version list box and then click the Update button. If a version range has been updated in the worksheet but not in the version, the Version Manager Index dialog box displays the version name in italics.

Creating Scenarios

From the Version Manager, we can attach the versions of the expenses range to scenarios. Here's how to attach the Current version to Scenario1 and the Future version to Scenario2:

1. In the Version Manager Index dialog box, select Current in the Version list box and click the Show button to display the Current version of the expenses range in the worksheet. Then click the Scenario button to display the Create Scenario dialog box. Click OK to accept the default names and settings for Scenario1.

2. Click the Scenario button again to create a second scenario. This time select Future in the Available Versions edit box and click the << button to enter EXPENSES.Future in the Selected Versions edit box. The dialog box now looks like this:

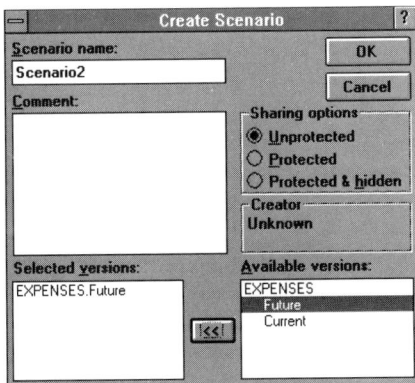

3. Click OK to close the Create Scenario dialog box and then click the Close button to close the Version Manager Index dialog box.

Changing Scenarios

By changing scenarios, we can display different versions of a worksheet to see the results of various conditions or assumptions. In the project cost estimate worksheet, we can use the scenarios we've created to show the effect of future facility costs on project costs and profit margin.

To make it easier to access the Version Manager, we will use the Version icon on the Goodies SmartIcon palette. If you continued on to this chapter from Chapter 4, this palette is already displayed at the top of your screen. Otherwise, you need to switch palettes.

1. Click the SmartIcon selector on the status bar. If Goodies is not highlighted in the SmartIcon palette list, select it now.

2. Click the Version icon to display the Version Manager Index dialog box with the OVERHEAD table in the background.

3. Select the Scenario2 and click the Show button. The expense amounts for Rent, Insurance, and Equipment in the overhead table change to the future values. (If you want, take a minute to toggle back and forth between Scenario1 and Scenario2 to see how the OVERHEAD table changes. When you are finished, display the Current values.)

4. Choose ESTIMATE.WK4 from the bottom of the Window menu and move the dialog box so that you can see the effect of this scenario on the project cost estimate. The Total Cost is $8,078.00 and the Profit Margin is $4,349.69.

Switching scenarios

5. Choose OVERHEAD.WK4 from the Window menu, select Scenario2, and click the Show button.

6. Return to the ESTIMATE window and check out the results. The Total Cost is now $8,318.00 and the Profit Margin is $4,478.92.

7. Close the Version Manager Index dialog box by clicking the Close button and save the ESTIMATE worksheet. Then save the OVERHEAD worksheet. (1-2-3 saves the version information with the file. If you don't save the file, the version changes will be lost.)

You now have a completed project estimate that takes into account overhead costs as well as the direct costs associated with the project. You also have a means of assessing the impact of varying overhead costs. You can easily set up versions and scenarios to examine the effects of other changes such as salary increases.

As we said at the beginning of the chapter, you can adapt this set of worksheets in many ways to help you quickly assemble bids. You can also use versions of these worksheets for such tasks as comparing the cost of doing projects in-house with estimates that you receive from vendors. And once you have set up a lookup table such as the employee information table, you can link it to worksheets that perform a variety of other personnel-related calculations.

6 Time-Saving Techniques

What you will learn

Biosphere Office Products
13478 S.W. 88th St.
Bellevue, WA 98111

SOLD BY			TERMS		SHIP VIA	FREIGHT TERMS
Item #	Qty.	Part #	Description		Unit Cost	Extended Cost
					Total	
					Tax	
					Shipping/Handling	
					Amount Due	

In this final chapter, we discuss techniques that can greatly increase your efficiency by automating some of the routine tasks associated with setting up worksheets. First, we show you how to assign a name to combinations of formatting so that you can apply all the formatting simply by applying the named style. Then we tackle macros. Once you see how easy it is to record keystrokes as macros in 1-2-3, even those of you whose palms get sweaty at the thought of having to deal with something as "techie" as a macro programming language will begin thinking of ways to put macros to use.

The example for this chapter is an invoice. In Chapter 3, we said we would show you a way to avoid having to manually input data into databases such as invoice logs. The key to streamlining the data-input process is to generate forms such as invoices in 1-2-3 and then use a macro to make 1-2-3 do the work of transferring the data from the invoices to the invoice log.

Setting Up an Invoice

The invoice we are going to create in this chapter is shown on the previous page. Take a quick look to get oriented, and then let's set up the invoice worksheet:

1. Open a new worksheet and save it as INVOICE.WK4.

2. Because the invoice will need a lot of formatting, display the Formatting SmartIcon palette by clicking the SmartIcon selector on the status bar and choosing Formatting from the list.

3. Make the following entries in the indicated cells, using the capitalization shown:

F1	ORDER DATE
G1	INVOICE NUMBER
F4	SHIP DATE
G4	PO NUMBER
D7	SOLD TO
F7	SHIP TO
A13	SOLD BY
D13	TERMS

F13	SHIP VIA
G13	FREIGHT TERMS
A15	Item #
B15	Qty.
C15	Part #
D15	Description
F15	Unit Cost
G15	Extended Cost
F30	Total
F31	Tax
F32	Shipping/Handling
F34	Amount Due

4. Use the Column Width command on the Style menu to adjust the column widths as follows:

A, B, C	6
D, F, G	18
E	1

5. Apply the Bold style to A13, D13, F13..G13, and F30..F34.

6. Center the entries in the range A15..G15.

7. Right-align cell D7 and the range F30..F34.

8. Apply the 12/31/93 date format to cells F2 and F5.

9. Finally, apply the Currency format to the ranges F16..F29 and G16..G34.

Using Named Styles

As you know, to apply a style to a selected cell or range, you can click the appropriate icon or you can choose the Font & Attributes command from the Style menu and select the font, size, and style in the Font & Attributes dialog box. On page 50, we discussed copying styles using the Copy Styles icon. Here we'll take a quick look at another formatting shortcut: named styles.

Once you establish a combination of styles for a particular cell or range, you can save that combination as a named style and then apply that combination of formatting to other ranges simply by selecting the name. Try out this feature by following these steps:

1. Select cell F1 and click the Bold icon.

2. Choose Lines & Color from the Style menu to display the Lines & Color dialog box:

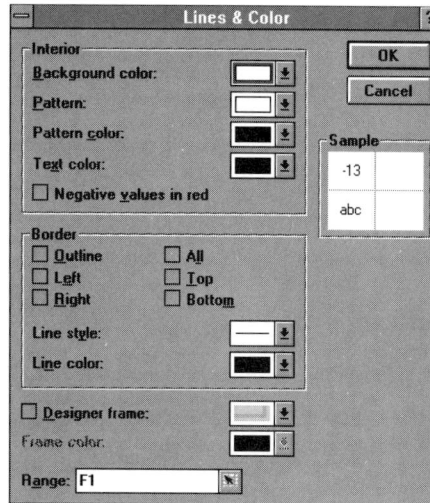

3. In the Interior section, click the down arrow at the right end of the Pattern edit box. 1-2-3 displays several options from which to choose. Select the pattern in the fourth column of the fourth row and click OK. As you can see here, the cell's background is now shaded with the selected pattern:

Modifying named styles

If you create a named style and then want to change its combination of formatting, select a cell to which you have applied the style, make the necessary formatting changes, and then choose Named Style from the Style menu. Select the style from the Existing Styles list, click the Define button, and click OK. 1-2-3 redefines the named style to incorporate the current formatting of the cell.

Next we'll create a named style for this combination of formatting:

1. With F1 still selected, choose Named Style from the Style menu. 1-2-3 displays this dialog box:

Creating named styles

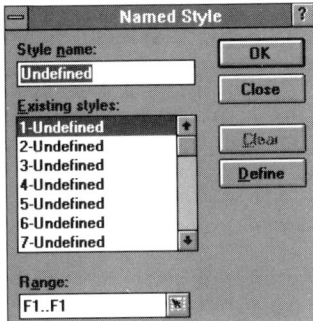

2. In the Style Name edit box, type *Heading 1*.

3. Click the Define button to save the formatting of the selected cell under the name Heading 1, and then click OK.

   Now let's apply the named style to a few of the other headings in the worksheet:

1. Select cell G1, choose Named Style from the Style menu, select Heading 1, and click OK. The text in G1 is now bold, and its background is shaded.

2. Select cell D7, hold down the Ctrl key, and select cell F7. Then click the *style selector*—the third box from the left in the status bar—to display the named styles you have defined for this worksheet—in this case, only Heading 1.

3. Select Heading 1 to apply its combination of styles.

4. Repeat steps 2 and 3 for the range F4..G4. Here are the results:

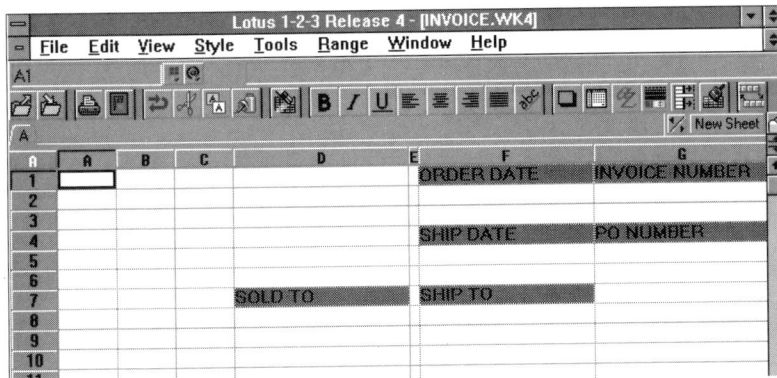

Deleting named styles

To delete a named style, select a cell to which you have applied the style and then choose the Named Style command from the Style menu. Select the style in the Existing Styles list, click the Clear button, and then click OK.

5. Click the Save icon to save the work you have done so far.

As you can see, named styles are a convenient way of duplicating formatting you have defined for one part of your worksheet in other parts. Another important shortcut technique is to create a macro to apply frequently used styles or formats. We'll try this technique in the next section.

Creating Macros

A macro is a set of instructions recorded in a column of a worksheet. When you run a macro, 1-2-3 moves sequentially down the column of instructions, doing whatever it is told to do. The 1-2-3 macro language includes two special kinds of instructions—macro key names and macro commands—both enclosed in curly braces, { and }.

Macro key names

- *Macro key names* represent menu commands and other operations that you perform from the keyboard. For example, {Alt} activates the menu bar, and {Up} moves the cell pointer up one cell in the worksheet.

Macro commands

- *Macro commands* generally perform more elaborate operations; for example, {Let} enters a value into a specified cell.

In addition to these instructions, a macro can contain literal character keystrokes. You'll see examples of all these elements in the macros we'll build in this chapter.

A macro is available for you to use whenever the worksheet that contains it is open, and you can use a macro stored in one open worksheet in any other open worksheet. When you create a macro, you normally assign it a special range name consisting of the backslash character and a letter of the alphabet—for example, \B. When you want to run this macro, you simply press Ctrl-B. 1-2-3 then finds the macro named \B and performs its instructions.

A rather sophisticated alternative is to write a macro and then assign it to a button. In this way, you can create the equivalent of SmartIcons to carry out the tasks you perform most frequently in your work with 1-2-3.

Macro libraries

You might want to build a library of general-purpose macros in a separate worksheet file. Assign the file a filename such as MACLIB.WK4 and open the file whenever you want to access the macros it contains. (For example, you might want to copy the Border, Outline, and Letterhead macros to this file for use in other worksheet projects.)

To make it easy for new users to start creating macros right away, 1-2-3 has a special tool called the *transcript window* for recording keystrokes and commands in macro format. In this window, 1-2-3 transcribes your keystrokes and commands into macro language instructions. This transcription process takes place only when you tell 1-2-3 to record your steps. To see the macro transcriptions of your most recent activity, you simply open the transcript window by choosing Macro and then Show Transcript from the Tools menu.

The transcript window

Our discussion of macros will be necessarily brief and is not intended to make you an instant 1-2-3 macro expert. The idea is to get you thinking about whether tasks you perform routinely could be more efficiently carried out with macros, and to give you enough information to explore the topic further on your own. We start by showing you how to copy a macro from the transcript window. Next we look at the process of creating macros from scratch. Then we examine a macro that transfers information from a filled-out invoice to an invoice log. And finally, we assign a macro to a button.

Using the Transcript Window

To resemble the invoice at the beginning of the chapter, the invoice now on your screen needs borders around several ranges. For this purpose, we'll create two different macros, which we'll call the Border macro and the Outline macro. The Border macro will put a thick border around each cell in a selected range. The Outline macro will draw a thick border around the perimeter of a selected range.

We'll begin this task by adding sheet B to the INVOICE worksheet. (You'll use this sheet to store all the macros you create in this chapter.) Then we'll open the transcript window. After we make selections from the Lines & Color dialog box to create the two kinds of borders, we'll copy the resulting macros directly from the transcript window to sheet B. Let's get going:

A separate macro sheet

1. Click the New Sheet button at the right end of the tab line to add sheet B to the INVOICE worksheet.

The Border macro

2. Enter the heading *Border Macro* in cell B:A1, click the Bold icon to display the heading in bold, and increase the width of column A to 50.

Opening the transcript window

3. From the Tools menu, choose Macro and then Show Transcript to display the transcript window.

4. Choose Tile from the Window menu to display the transcript and worksheet windows side by side.

The Macro Builder SmartIcon palette

5. Use the SmartIcon selector on the status bar to choose the Macro Builder palette. Your screen now looks like this:

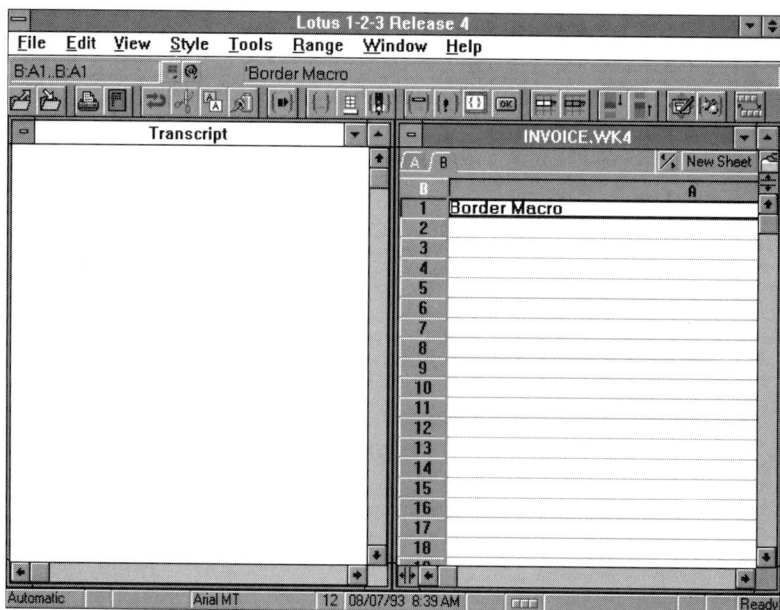

6. Take a moment to right-click each icon and read its description in the title bar before moving on.

For convenience, we'll apply borders to the cells of sheet B while we develop the two macros. Then when the macros are complete, we'll return to sheet A and use the macros to apply the borders to the invoice. Follow these steps:

Turning on the macro recorder

1. Turn on the macro recorder by clicking the Record Macro icon. The word Rec appears in the status bar to let you know that all your steps will be recorded in the transcript window.

2. Choose Lines & Color from the Style menu to display the Lines & Color dialog box.

3. In the Border section, click the All option. Then click the down arrow at the right end of the Line Style edit box, select the bold line (the third one down) from the drop-down list, and click OK.

4. Turn off the macro recorder by clicking the Record Macro icon. The word Rec disappears from the status bar, and your screen now looks like this:

Turning off the macro recorder

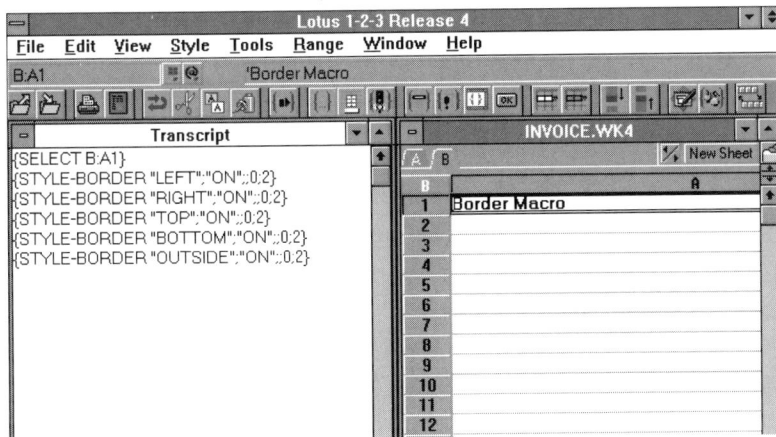

The instructions in the transcript window correspond to the selections you have just made in the Lines & Color dialog box. Now is a good time to move the macro to sheet B:

1. In the transcript window, select all but the first row of instructions.

2. Click the Copy icon to copy the selection to the Clipboard.

3. In the worksheet window, select cell B:A2 and click the Paste icon to paste the copy of the macro in sheet B.

4. With B:A2 still selected, choose Name from the Range menu. Type \B (a backslash followed by the letter B) as the name for this cell, and click OK.

That's it for the Border macro. Now let's follow a similar procedure to create the Outline macro.

Using the keyboard to choose commands

You have probably become accustomed to using the mouse to make menu selections, but keep in mind that you can also use the keyboard. For example, you can press the Alt key followed by S and then L to choose the Lines & Color command from the Style menu.

1. Select cell B:A8, leaving one blank cell between the first macro and the new macro you are about to create. (When 1-2-3 encounters a blank cell in a macro column, it assumes it has reached the end of the macro.)

2. Enter the heading *Outline Macro*. Make the heading bold by choosing Font & Attribute from the Style menu and clicking Bold. (We use this method because the Bold icon is not available on the Macro Builder SmartIcon palette.)

Clearing the transcript window 3. Activate the transcript window and choose Clear All from the Edit menu to clear the current contents of the window.

4. In the worksheet window, select cell B:A8 and click the Record Macro icon.

5. Choose Lines & Color from the Style menu. In the Lines & Color dialog box, select the Outline option and then select the bold line from the Line Style drop-down list box. Click OK. A new sequence of macro instructions appears in the transcript window.

6. Click the Record Macro icon to turn off the recorder.

7. In the transcript window, select all but the first line of the contents of the window and click the Copy icon.

8. In the worksheet window, select cell B:A9 and click the Paste icon to paste the second macro in sheet B. Then with B:A9 still selected, choose Name from the Range menu, and assign the name \O (a backslash followed by the letter *O*) to the cell. Click OK.

Closing the transcript window 9. You are now finished with the transcript window, so click the Transcript Window icon to close the window, and then click the worksheet window's Maximize button to expand the worksheet to fill the screen. Your worksheet contains these macros:

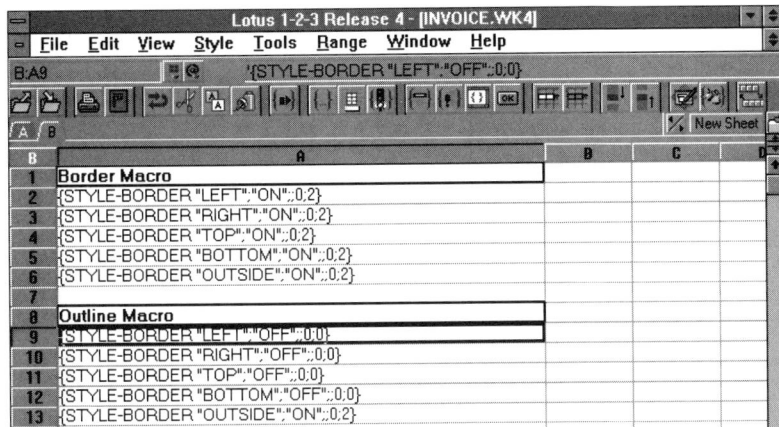

Running Macros

Now you are ready to test these two macros on the invoice. Because you have assigned the names \B and \O to the macros, you can run them simply by pressing Ctrl-B or Ctrl-O from the keyboard. Here goes:

1. Click tab A to display sheet A.

2. Select A:F1..A:G2 and press Ctrl-B. 1-2-3 puts a border around each cell in the range. Repeat this step for the range A:F4..A:G5.

3. Now select A:A8..A:D11 and press Ctrl-O. 1-2-3 puts a border around the perimeter of the selected range. Repeat this step for the range A:F8..A:G11, and then press Home so that you can see these results:

Running macros from the transcript window

If you want to create and use a macro for a temporary situation, you can create the macro in the transcript window and run it from that window. You do this by creating the macro with the macro recorder, selecting the lines of the macro, and then clicking the Transcript Playback icon, which is to the right of the Paste icon when you are in the transcript window. When you run a macro in this way, the macro commands apply to the worksheet and cell that was active when you entered the transcript window.

Both macros are working correctly, so let's use them to outline some more ranges:

1. Select A13..C14 and press Ctrl-O.

2. Select the following ranges in turn and press Ctrl-O after each selection:

A:A16..A:A29	A:D16..A:E29
A:B16..A:B29	A:F13..A:F14
A:C16..A:C29	A:F16..A:F29
A:D13..A:E14	A:G13..A:G14
A:D15..A:E15	A:G16..A:G29

3. Select the following cells or ranges in turn and press Ctrl-B after each selection:

A:D7	A:A15..A:C15
A:F7	A:F15..A:G15
A:G34	A:G30..A:G32

Turning off grid lines

4. To make the borders stand out, choose Set View Preferences from the View menu, deselect the Grid Lines option (there should be no X in its check box), and click OK. Press Home to see the results:

Macro availability

A macro is available for use in either of two situations: when you open the worksheet in which the macro is stored, or when you assign a macro to a custom icon on a SmartIcon palette. See the tip on page 149 for more information.

5. Now would be a good time to save the worksheet again to preserve the work you have done so far, so click the Save icon.

You might want to take a minute or two to look at the macros you have created and see what you can make of the way 1-2-3 translates menu actions into macro instructions. Click tab B to view the two macros. They consist primarily of literal character keystrokes enclosed in curly braces. For example, STYLE-BORDER is the equivalent of pulling down the Style menu, choosing the Lines & Color command, and selecting the Border options. The next part of the macro—LEFT, RIGHT, and so forth—represents the border sides. The rest of the macro shows the settings for each border, with 2 representing your Line Style selection—the second option down from the default, which is 0. In the Outline Macro, OUTSIDE is the only border turned on.

A thorough examination of 1-2-3's macro instructions is beyond the scope of this book. Suffice it to say that instructions exist for just about every worksheet task you can perform. The 1-2-3 Help system includes detailed information about macros, so to learn more about macros in general and about specific macro instructions, choose Macros from the Help menu.

Help with macros

Defining Macros from Scratch

You've probably noticed the blank hole in the top left corner of the invoice in sheet A. Let's create a simple macro that will insert a company name and address in this area. In the process, you'll learn a little more about the 1-2-3 macro language. Follow these steps:

1. On worksheet B, select cell B:A15, enter the heading *Letterhead Macro*, and make the heading bold. (If you feel more comfortable working with grid lines turned on at this point, simply choose the Set View Preferences command from the View menu, click the Grid Lines option, and then click OK.)

The Letterhead macro

2. To enter the company name and address, turn the page and type the macro instructions in B:A16..B:A23 just as you see them, except that you will probably want to substitute your own company's name and address. You don't have to type the comments in column B, which explain the action of each instruction.

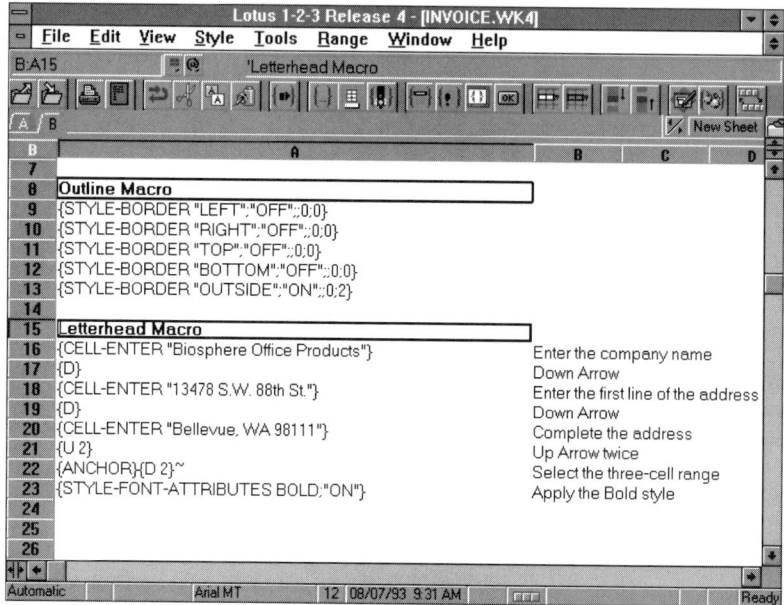

Be sure to type a space between U and 2 and between D and 2. Also, notice the use of the tilde character (~), which is the equivalent of pressing Enter in a macro.

3. Select cell B:A16, choose Name from the Range menu, and assign the name \L (a backslash and the letter *L*) to this macro.

Now let's test the new macro:

1. Click tab A to view sheet A.

2. With cell A1 selected, press Ctrl-L to run the new macro. Then press Down Arrow to see the result:

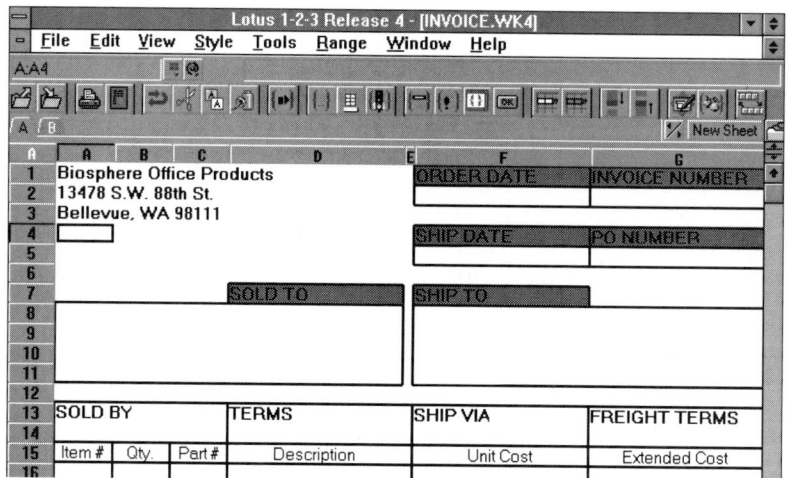

Congratulations. You've just written your first macro.

Logging Invoice Data with a Macro

You now know enough about macros to follow along as we create one that will take the information you enter into the invoice (sheet A) and record it in an invoice log. This macro can be adapted for many uses. For example, you could use the techniques you learned while creating the invoice to develop a contacts template. You could then adapt the macro to pull information about each new client you work with into a name and address database. Or you might want to create an expense-report template and adapt the macro to record expenses in a reimbursement summary.

Before we can work on the macro, we need to create the invoice log sheet, so let's get started.

Setting Up an Invoice Log

For demonstration purposes, we'll keep this log very simple. Follow these steps:

1. Click tab B to display sheet B. Then click the New Sheet button to add sheet C to the INVOICE.WK4 file.

2. Make the following entries in the indicated cells on the new sheet:

C:A1	INVOICE LOG
C:A3	Date
C:B3	Invoice Number
C:C3	Salesperson
C:D3	Amount of Sale

3. Select C:A1..D3 and apply the Bold style by choosing Font & Attributes from the Style menu and clicking the Bold option. Then select C:A1..C:D1 and center the heading by choosing Alignment from the Style menu and clicking Center and Across Columns in the Horizontal section.

4. Adjust the column widths so that you can see all the entries.

5. We want 1-2-3 to append new invoices to the end of the invoice log, so select cell C:A4, choose Name from the Range

> **Template worksheets**
>
> When you create a worksheet, like the invoice, that you want to use over and over again, it's important that you save the worksheet with a different name before filling in any details. That way, you preserve the original blank worksheet template for future use. In the case of the invoice, you might want to use the invoice numbers as filenames for specific invoices and keep the name INVOICE for the template.

menu, and assign the name END to the selected cell. Then press the Home key to move to the top of the sheet, which looks like this:

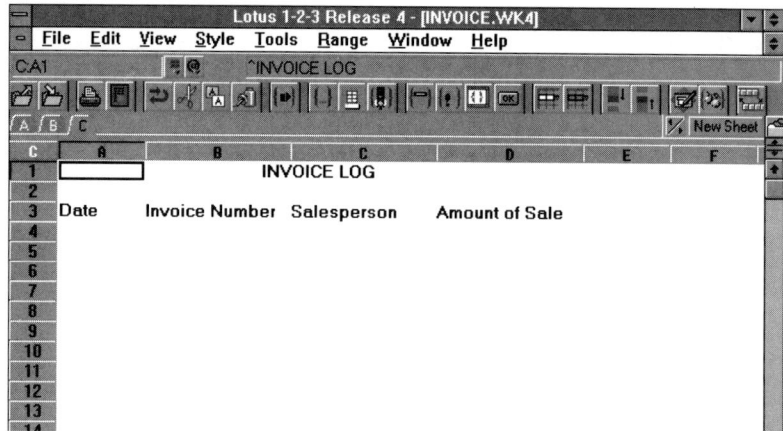

6. Return to sheet A and use the Name command to assign the following names to the specified cells:

A:F2	ORDERDATE
A:G2	INVNUM
A:A14	SOLDBY
A:G34	AMOUNT

7. Click the Save icon to save the worksheet.

That's it for the log. Now let's move on to create the macro.

Creating the Invoice Log Macro

The Invoice Log macro we are going to create uses a macro command called {Let} to copy data items from the named cells in sheet A to sheet C. You'll also see examples of the @CELLPOINTER function, which identifies the address of the current cell.

The Invoice Log macro

1. Click tab B, and in sheet B enter the following macro in the range B:A25..B:A37 (again, you don't have to type the comments in column B):

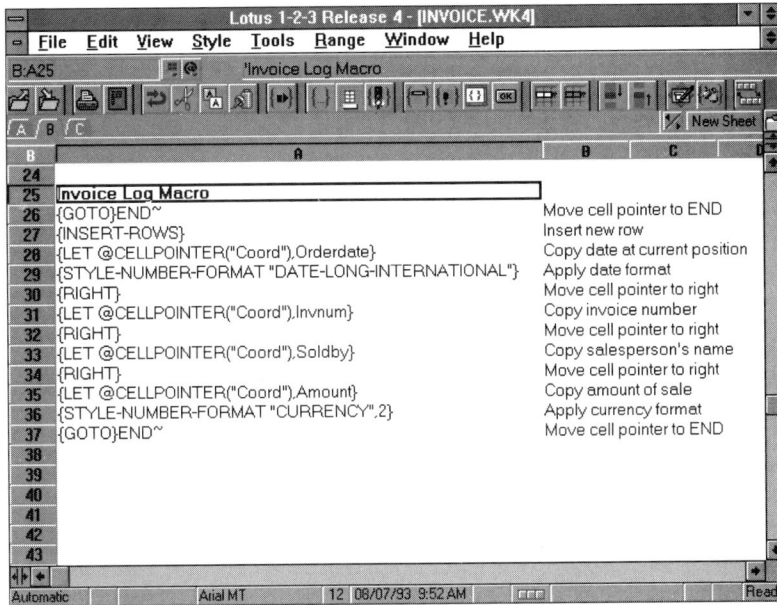

2. Select cell B:A26, and choose Name from the Range menu. Assign the name \I (a backslash and the letter *I*) to this cell.

3. Click the Save icon.

Running the Macro

Now for the acid test. We'll make a few entries in the invoice on sheet A and then run the macro. Here goes:

1. In sheet A, make the following entries in the indicated cells and then press Home:

A:F2	09/09/93
A:G2	5234AA
A:A14	Karnov, Peter
A:G34	54687

2. Choose Split from the View menu, click Perspective, and deselect the Synchronize option so that you can scroll different parts of the window independently. Click OK to view sheets A, B, and C all at once.

Viewing multiple sheets

3. With sheet A active, press Ctrl-I. If you have entered the macro correctly, 1-2-3 transfers the information you entered in the invoice to the log, as shown on the next page.

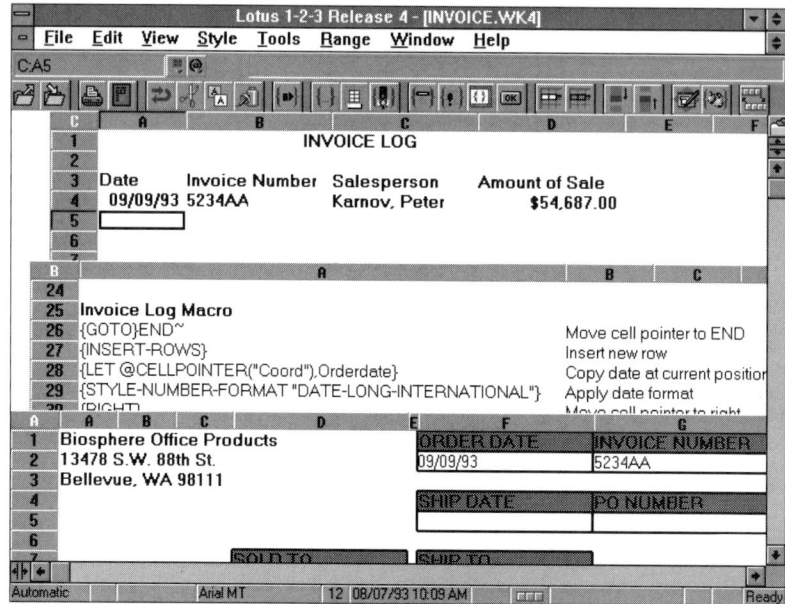

You might want to enter new values in sheet A and then press Ctrl-I to run the macro again to see how 1-2-3 appends the information from successive invoices to the invoice log.

Assigning Macros to Buttons

As we mentioned earlier, you can assign a macro to a button on the worksheet and run the macro simply by clicking the button. Buttons provide instant access to your macros and serve as a graphic reminder of a macro's availability. In this section, we'll use the Button icon to create a button that represents the Invoice Log macro. Follow these steps:

1. Change the invoice entries in sheet A as follows and then press Home:

A:F2	10/12/93
A:G2	5784AA
A:A14	Karnov, Peter
A:G34	32621

Creating buttons

2. Click the Button icon and draw a button in the top left corner of sheet C. (Don't worry about the exact size; you can adjust it later.) 1-2-3 displays the Assign to Button dialog box:

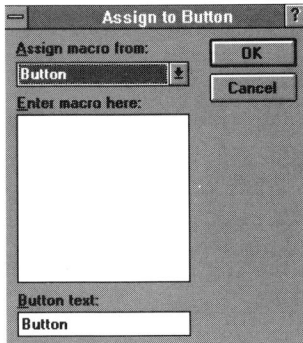

3. Click the down arrow at the right end of the Assign Macro From edit box and select Range from the drop-down list.

4. The Existing Named Ranges list box now displays the names assigned in this worksheet. Click \I to select the range name of the Invoice Log macro.

5. In the Button Text edit box, type *Transfer* as the label for the button, and click OK. The button now looks like this:

Customizing button labels

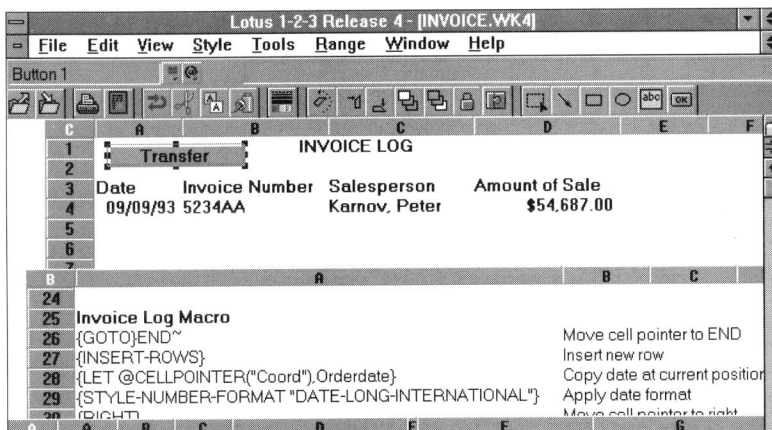

6. If you need to resize the button, grab any of its handles and reshape it. Drag the button if you need to reposition it.

   Now we'll test the button on the invoice worksheet:

1. Click anywhere in sheet C to clear the button handles and then click the Transfer button. 1-2-3 executes the Invoice Log macro and adds the invoice information we entered earlier to the log, which now looks like this.

SmartIcon macros

You can assign a macro to a custom SmartIcon and display the new icon in a SmartIcon palette. Choose the SmartIcon command from the Tools menu, click the Edit Icon button, set up an icon with the macro in the Edit Icon dialog box, and add the icon to the palette of your choice. Then whenever you want to run the macro, you can simply click the icon on that palette.

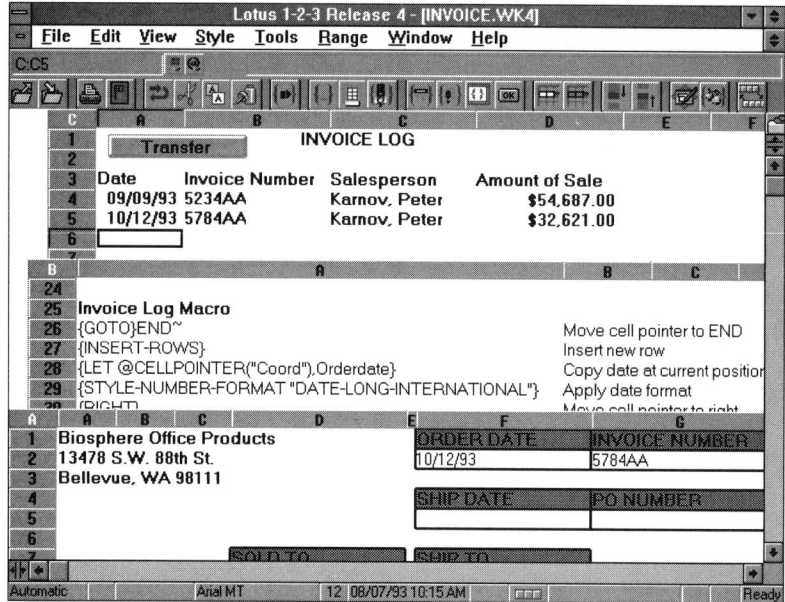

The button is a permanent part of the INVOICE worksheet. If you need to change or delete it, right-click the button and choose the appropriate command from its quick menu.

If the Macro Doesn't Work

If 1-2-3 encounters a recognizable error in the macro, it stops and displays a message announcing the location of the error. The most likely cause of errors is typos. On the other hand, 1-2-3 might complete a macro without interruption but produce unexpected results. In the latter case, 1-2-3 offers a way to sleuth out the cause of the problem. Choose Macro from the Tools menu to display this cascade menu from which you can access two macro debugging tools:

Icons for SmartIcons

You can use any of the icons that come with 1-2-3 for your macros—they're located in the SHEETICO subdirectory of the 123R4W\PROGRAM directory. You can also create your own icons, either within 1-2-3 or in a graphics program. Choose Smart-Icons from the Tools menu to display the SmartIcons dialog box and then click the Edit Icon button to display the Edit Icon dialog box. Here you can edit existing icons, create new icons, or paste in an icon that you have placed on the Clipboard.

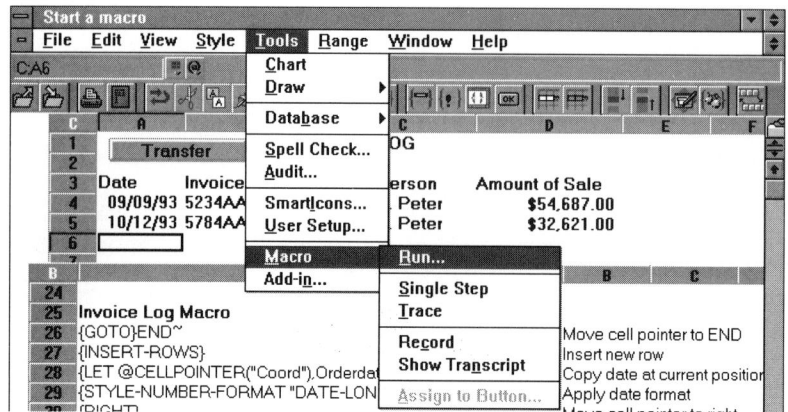

Choosing Single Step allows you to step through the macro one instruction at a time. Choosing Single Step and then Trace allows you to view this Macro Trace box during the macro's performance:

Macro Trace	
B:A37	{GOTO}END▮

As you can see, the Macro Trace box displays the location of the current macro instruction, along with the instruction itself. To step from one macro instruction to the next, press any key. 1-2-3 highlights the instructions as it carries them out, giving you the opportunity to see the macro in slow motion and spot errors. You turn off Single Step and Trace by choosing their respective commands from the Macro cascade menu to remove the check marks to the left of their command names. (You can also turn these debugging tools on and off by clicking their icons on the Macro Builder SmartIcon palette.)

Well, that quick overview of macros winds up the book. You are now equipped with the tools you need to create some pretty sophisticated worksheets and should be familiar enough with 1-2-3 to explore the more complex features on your own.

Index